from
the
HICKORY
STICK

Budgie Hallamor

Splinters from the HICKORY STICK

by

ELIZABETH HOLLAMON

A few million words
about the adventures of
running a private school

THE
WATERCRESS
PRESS

San Antonio
1998

First Edition

Cover by Paul Hudgins
Illustrations by Carlotta Barker

An Evett-Geron Associates book
from
The Watercress Press

Additional copies of this book may be ordered from:
E. E. Hollamon
902 N. Austin Street
Seguin, Texas

LC#98-75197
ISBN# 0-934955-37-9

Dedicated

to

Wini Answell—Ole Tonto

who for nearly a quarter century typed,

re-spelled, and mailed

pretty nearly on time The Hickory Sticks.

She also tried valiantly to rephrase The Sticks

with a view to keeping me out of the courts.

Most of the time she was successful.

CONTENTS

Once Upon A Time

Once upon a time — has there ever been a better beginning? — an old friend called in the middle of the night and asked if I was interested in being headmistress of a small Episcopal school on an island in the Gulf of Mexico.

Greater lunacy I had rarely encountered in responsible people. I told her "No!" in unconditional terms.

Three weeks later I found myself accepting the position. The whole scenario could have been written by the Marx Brothers. I was leaving for Europe with twenty-five college students to be gone six weeks. I had to resign my job in such carefully chosen words that Houston Independent School District might reconsider my resignation in case I flunked Private School 101. Then there was moving, storing furniture, and explaining this seeming lapse of sanity to friends and family in four days.

The pace hasn't really slowed in the last quarter century. The headmistress gig seems to be made of about equal parts of elation, disappointment, achievement, failure, chicken and feathers. It's had more ups and downs than The Rattler. It's been bare-knuckle fun, and I wouldn't trade it for a barrel of diamonds.

The Hickory Stick

A couple of years after I became Headmistress of Trinity Episcopal School in Galveston, the Southwest Association of Episcopal Schools (SAES) invited me to become a member of the Executive Board. Lacking qualified candidates, they chose me President two years after that.

One of the perks of the job was that I got to write a column monthly for *The Texas Churchman* about schools. A clergy friend on the Board asked what I intended to call my column, and when I confessed I'd never given that part a thought he began singing the old ditty we all remember from childhood. Well, those of us old enough remember it. It went:

Reading and 'Riting and 'Rithmetic
Taught to the tune of a hickory stick.

That did it. For the next twenty-five years, once a month, ready or not, the "Hickory Stick" hit the street. Most of the time in the early years it really was about schools, but then as I got older and some of my insulation wore thin it became more and more a vehicle for my monthly temper tantrum. Nobody seemed to mind. The fan mail kept coming.

I left the Diocese of Texas, and *The Texas Churchman* when I went to Texas Military Institute as its first headmistress in its 105-year history, but there were other publications to which I had access. The diatribes continued. Finally, after my fourth retirement, I decided to stop writing and start recycling.

This book isn't the lot by a long shot. If it goes, we could always pick some more and do *Son of Hickory Stick*, or *Hickory Stick Revisited*. And if those were successful I suppose I could always write some new ones. There is plenty of material at hand, but Ole Tonto, my faithful secretary, isn't here to edit them. Well, there must be somebody out there who knows how to spell. It sure isn't me.

The Seventies

In the beginning was the word . . .
The Gospel of John

1

THE MOUTH OF THE GUADALUPE FLOWETH. I'VE WANDERED AROUND SPOUTING WISDOM THIS MORNING WHILE I RECYCLED A PAIR OF STOCKINGS. THE ENVIRONMENT WAS NOT IMPROVED.

I spoke to the Daughters of the Republic of Texas on the occasion of the centennial of The Cradle. That's kind of the home office of the Daughters. I was acceptably brief. It was a Sunday afternoon in September and the Oilers were playing. Then I had a few words for the troops at the SAES Conference in Little Rock. That was an especially good conference and I can say that from a wealth of experience since I've been to that do more times than most of the participants have been to communion. Teachers just keep on getting younger. Notice that? I look at some of the parents who walk in my office and think it's immoral for them to have children at their age.

This weekend I'm setting up the tent in Waco for the 35th birthday of St. Paul's School, one of the pioneer and premier schools in our diocese. I'm flattered to be asked to be their speaker.

As I dined handsomely on airline peanuts coming home last Saturday, I wondered how all this came about. If you pedal as hard as I have for the past many years, watching the road to try to avoid chugholes instead of reading the map, you often find yourself at a destination and wonder how in blazes you ever arrived there. I bet Moses felt the same way. Face it. A wilderness is a wilderness, said Gertrude Stein.

The answer is, I got there through Episcopal Schools.

3

Some twenty years ago, *The Texas Churchman* asked me to write a column on the schools of the Church. I got the tap because I'd recently been elected president of Southwestern Association of Episcopal Schools. I think Lucy Germany had one column in mind. With great bravado I entitled the column "Hickory Stick" in honor of the old song about schools, and began sending them in regularly. Lucy was too gracious to ask me to cease and desist.

Let's see. That's twelve columns times twenty years. Two hundred forty pieces of monthly opinion. Okay. So I missed the deadline on some. Make it two and a quarter. On the other hand, I've got about that many I never sent in. The local saying is that some folks go home after a hard day and kick the cat. Budgie writes a "Hickory Stick." Most of those "Hickory Sticks" will remain blessedly unpublished — like the one I wrote on the conduct of the United States Senate as they performed in the center ring of the Confirmation Circus.

It's amazing how many people read *The Texas Episcopalian*, or whatever we call ourselves now, and of those, how many read the "Hickory Stick." I hear from somebody every month — not always somebody who agrees, but in each case their comments are well phrased. Once a teacher, always a teacher. I have one friend at 815 Second Avenue, New York City, that I hear from monthly. He's a fan. I've heard from a lady in Alaska, a lady in Kansas, an Admissions Officer at the Virginia Seminary, and even from some local friends in Washington. That one's duly framed. I wonder how a diocesan paper covers so much territory. Wonder and rejoice, that is.

I've even had a couple from the Archbishop of Canterbury, but they weren't fan letters. They just said that he couldn't come to Galveston that week. Archbishops of Canterbury sign their names funny, but I framed them anyway because they read, "Dear Miss Hollamon." If they'd said, "Dear Budgie," I'd have bronzed them. It's a good thing they had a Lambeth Palace heading or I wouldn't have known who it was from. Ever hear of Robert Cantbrian? At least I think that's what it says. Reckon that has any direct bearing on the old adage, "Never give 'em your right name"?

Ah, the ramblings of old age. In Little Rock, I billed myself as the oldest living graduate with a ten handicap, but I lied. It's really twelve. Whatever. When you reach that milepost and realize how you got there — and how much fun you're having upon arrival — there's not but one thing to say. Thank you. Thank you for agreeing. Thank you for disagreeing, but most of all thank you for reading.

2

I HAVE A SUPERSTITION CONCERNING THE OPENING OF SCHOOL. TRINITY SCHOOL HAS OPENED NINE TIMES DURING MY TENURE. SEVEN OF THOSE WERE IN THE MIDDLE OF A REALLY NOTEWORTHY STORM. THEY WERE ALL GOOD YEARS. ONCE, PRIOR TO THIS YEAR, I DID OPEN IN SUNSHINE. THE YEAR WAS TOTALLY DISASTER-RIDDEN, RANGING IN SEVERITY FROM TEACHER PROBLEMS TO HAVING THE MAY FETE RAINED OUT. YOU CAN COUNT ON THE FACT THAT I SPEND THE DAYS BEFORE SCHOOL OPENS HOLDING A NOVENA FOR MODERATE RAINS AND SHOWERS.

This year I must have been using the old prayer book because the day dawned sunny and hot. It's been downhill ever since. So far, I have had one teacher fail to make it back for the opening of school because she was caught in the Nicaraguan Revolution, and another fall off her shoe while walking down a flat sidewalk and break her leg. Not even prayer and fasting can save one from calamities like that. So that's the reason I am late with this frazzling column, and I hope it arrives before the deadline.

The flood of mail that crosses an administrator's desk this time of year goes mostly unread because of the demands of time, but should one be insomniac and have these educational offerings handy through some long and sleepless night, you will find them incredible. They contain all the fashionable falsehoods of our time. These falsehoods thrive in many publications. There is a kind of ideology that protects and nurtures them, and, as Hannah Arendt has observed, nothing inoculates the mind against truth as well as

6

ideology. It can be hard ideology like fascism, or soft ideology derived only from indolence and popular conventions, yet it can block truth.

When we do not carefully examine the prevailing untruths in education, we often abandon ourselves and our students to the loudest and most often repeated opinions rather than the most discerning ones. Thus spake William J. Bennett in *The Wall Street Journal.* I began working on his theory and was amazed at the number of fashionable falsehoods I could come up with before I even had to pause for breath.

Try this one. It's gone unchallenged for years. "One man's opinion is necessarily as good as another man's." As an unqualified statement, that is simply not true. My opinion on foreign affairs is not as good as that of Cyrus Vance because I do not have the facts necessary to make the judgment. I fear that Dr. Cooley would give scant attention to my medical opinion for the same reason. Why, then, do we persist in this falsehood? Because it's fashionable to pay lip service to such high democratic principle.

How about this one. "All men are created equal . . ." The next sentence in that document explains what Jefferson was alluding to, but no one ever quotes the next sentence. This has led to a fallacy that has almost ruined education and threatens to ruin the country. All men are created equal in the sight of God, and there, Buddy Boy, it stops. Jefferson would have had a seizure had he been allowed to see the result of his rhetoric. You may recall that, despite his democratic writing, Jefferson considered himself just a tad more equal than the rest of us. All men are not created equal. They have neither the same talents nor the same abilities, and it is incredible that we should keep mouthing this obvious fallacy.

How about, "There is no such thing as standard English these days. Whatever is in local use is considered correct." Horse feathers! Whether anyone chooses to publicly acknowledge it or not, standard English remains standard English — even though the fine points are growing a little fuzzy from disuse. People are judged on their use of standard English in every endeavor. How many businesses do you think are going to respond to a letter of application with incorrect spelling and little or no punctuation? Not to demand correct use of our language in schools is tantamount to a denial of rights in my book. It is a sin of omission for which schools should — and shortly will, I suspect — be held accountable.

For one of the current top ten I present for your listening and dancing pleasure this classic: "It is more important to teach values than facts." They cannot be separated. One who makes a value choice without knowing the facts chooses in ignorance and is irresponsible.

Also among the top ten is the hue and cry of those who call their children creative. That cry is that the outmoded practice of memorizing fact should be abandoned in favor of the more humane practice of enlarging fact with imagination. I think that's just marvelous. In some classes — I refuse to call them disciplines — they even get by with it. Some art has been accepted as outstanding that pays no attention whatever to the laws of perspective or any other accepted tenet. I applaud either their ability or their showmanship. Now, let's apply that creativity to say, geography. If one wishes to go from St. Louis to New Orleans by water, regardless of how innovative he may be, it has been found that one really ought to stick to the Mississippi River.

And for my grand finale, with lights flashing and trumpets blaring, I present: "You can't make students do what they don't want to do." Balderdash. Of course you can. Sometimes it takes a little longer than one would wish. Bertrand Russell said it years ago. "A civilized community must demand, on some occasions, that children behave in a manner which is not natural to them." That's the reason for school — to train the young in the way of civilization. To require training is no disgrace. Perhaps it's another fashionable falsehood to think that we all sprang forth fully trained and could not possibly be improved upon. But then, as Mr. Justice Holmes observed, the intellectual world is no more free of fashions and trends than any other.

Also prevalent in the ranks of headmistresses with typewriters is the fashionable falsehood that the entire world is marching doggedly to hell and the educational contingent is leading the parade. But the fact is that during the span of one lifetime, we have gone from horse and buggies to space shuttles. On the basis of this, it is not unreasonable to assume that civilization — even education — may muddle through and survive. It isn't unreasonable, but it isn't very fashionable either.

3

THE POPE ALIGHTED FROM HIS JAZZY JET IN HIS PRISTINE WHITE ROBE AND KISSED THE GROUND. THE HEADMISTRESS STUMBLED OFF A DILAPIDATED DELTA IN HER RUMPLED DENIM SKIRT AND COULDN'T FIND THE GROUND. HE HAD CHARMED MILLIONS. I HAD BEEN CHARMED BY NINE, BUT I'M SURE WE WERE BOTH PLEASED AND RELIEVED TO BE HOME. I ASSUME HE GOT HOME WITH ALL HIS RETINUE. I BROUGHT THE SAME NINE KIDS BACK FROM WASHINGTON THAT I HAD LEFT WITH. APPARENTLY WE PRAY TO THE SAME GOD.

The occasion was Mini-mester. It's sort of like educational recess. For a week in the spring we all light votive candles to John Dewey and opt for on-the-job learning. I am not John Dewey's greatest admirer. As a steady diet, caviar will never take the place of cornbread and Dewey will never take the place of McGuffey, but a change does sharpen the appetite. However, I freely confess to you that the reason I designed Mini-mester last year was not educational. It was cosmetic. In this day of tight money and carefully chosen priorities, private schools need a little window dressing. One ought to be a little showier than the competition or, as my late father was prone to say, "You don't run a horse on the big track in mule tack."

A week out of the classroom may be a little questionable, but it won't leave bruises and it makes marvelous conversation at the Racquet Club. So with these vaunted sentiments tacitly understood, I began planning Mini-mester. It read well. Camping at the Y.O. Ranch, a Texas history trip, sewing, kites, ornithology, photography, and the real biggie-do, a trip to Washington, D.C., to see how the government ran. Big Mama drew that bean.

Rarely has Washington been seen so thoroughly in such a limited period of time. We hit everything from the Capitol to the Cathedral and from the pandas to the Potomac. The kids were energetic and I was exhausted. I considered giving my body to science, but in the condition it was in I knew science would give it back.

The rigors of tour directing are not new to me. I've been through travel trauma O.C.S. In the course of taking some 300 teenagers to Europe over the last ten years I have suffered almost all the slings and arrows of outrageous fortune. I have looked up at a departing Rhine steamer to see two of my scatterbrained girls (who had reboarded to retrieve a raincoat, I later found out) steaming serenely toward Amsterdam. We, unfortunately, were headed toward Heidelberg.

I have had one over-conscientious young lady care-fully lock her passport in a hotel safety deposit box — and then lose the key at the beach in Cannes on Sunday after-noon. Of course we were leaving early Monday morning. The decision was whether to (a) hold up the whole thirty-five-man tour for a day while waiting for workmen to drill the box on Monday, (b) leave the child there unattended and go with the group, or (c) take her without passport and try to smuggle her across the French/Italian border. For two box tops and five dollars I'll tell you how I brought her home safely.

Then there is the Case of the Abandoned Camera. "Do not leave your passport in a camera case on the floor by the table in a sleazy sidewalk cafe in Dubrovnik," I said to them, "for assuredly it will be stolen and I will not be able to get you back aboard ship." Within thirty minutes of the lecture this well-traveled son of a Houston oil executive had followed the scenario to the letter and was without

11

reboarding pass or passport. It took sweet tones, smiles and lagniappe to get him past the harbor officials. Have you ever thought how you would tell a mother that you lost her kid in Yugoslavia and you're sure sorry?

The real showstopper, however, was the year I had the kid dive into the Arno River — and miss. He was impressing his date. Apparently he had not looked closely at what they had done to the sloping banks of the Arno after the Big Flood. They encased them in thirty feet of concrete — that's what they did. A swan dive into thirty feet of concrete smarts. The experiment proved conclusively that communication by the grunt-and-point system of linguistic endeavor can be effective. In the Florence emergency room they still think I speak fluent Italian.

With a background like this, honchoing my nine angels around Washington was a piece of cake. I even had time to watch how the children were reacting to their trip, and that's when I noticed a metamorphosis taking place. They began to change from a class at Trinity to separate, considerate, intelligent little individuals. They didn't wear the same personalities they had worn at school. Perhaps neither did I. Sure, they were still kids. There was a spate of lost cameras and a few furtive punches thrown. One got himself locked in the bathroom at the Mayflower and we had to call the hotel engineer to get him out, but that, my children, is the reason Jesus made hotel engineers. By and large they minded very well.

As time went on they not only minded, they responded. Their joyful reaction to the beauty of the city, the glory of their heritage, and the multitude of educational stimuli surrounding them was a delight to watch. Among the most delightful things seen was that the kid who had never been first at any academic thing at Trinity began to keep up with, and then outshine the others. By Thursday he was absolutely incandescent.

A young Congressional aide told me that they had

entertained another group from a well-known and respected school. Those children were older. She said they were extremely intelligent and equally arrogant. Her remarks ended with, "Yours are well prepared and a whole lot nicer. I'd rather have your children." I had too.

I'm sorry you're dead, Dewey. I would like to apologize in person. It is just possible that your theories might, after all, have some validity — on a limited basis, of course.

4

S T. PAUL AND I HAVE SEVERAL THINGS IN COMMON. WE WRITE THE LONGEST RUN-ON SENTENCES IN THE ENGLISH-SPEAKING WORLD. NEITHER OF US IS OVERBURDENED WITH PATIENCE, AND WE PERCEIVE OURSELVES AS HAVING TRIBULATIONS. I FIND IT DIFFICULT TO REMEMBER PAUL'S, BUT I CAN TELL YOU MINE. MY BABY GREAT-NIECE, KINSEY, JUST SPIT CARROTS ALL OVER MY BRAND-NEW-NEVER-BEFORE-DONNED SILK SWEATER. I DON'T THINK IT IS GOING TO COME OUT. I'VE SCRUBBED AS DILIGENTLY AS I SMILINGLY CAN AND VESTIGES STILL REMAIN.

Best I can recall, the epistle this week read, "In whatever state I find myself I am content." At least that's what it used to say before they translated it modernly. I have one question for Peripatetic Paul. Did any of your family ever spit carrots on your new sweater? How content were you?

It brings to mind a wonderful short story by James Thurber, "If Grant Had Been Drunk at Appomattox." What if St. Paul had had carrots spit up on his new white toga on the way to Ephesus? The whole literature of Christianity might have been altered.

What if St. Andrew had said, "*Hold it*, fellows. I have traveled for this company on a tourist-class ticket through Greece and Russia and Scotland. I could write a book on the acts I've been through, but I simply don't *do* upside-down crucifixions."

Suppose St. Peter had said, "Quo Vadis? Let me tell you about Vadis. The minute I saw those Romans begin filling a dance card between the Christians and the lions, I determineth to depart from Dodge. That's Quo Vadis."

What if St. John had said, "*Patmos*! Have you ever *been* to Patmos? You can't get a decent night's lodging anywhere. Last time, I had to stay at the Mountaintop Monastery. Their pillows were like stone. Someday I'll tell you about the dreams I had sleeping on *those* pillows."

But back to the real world. We often speak of Christians as a family, and we should, because ideally that's what we are, but I sometimes think we ignore the obligations to our own family while we are out collecting strays in the name of good works. You can always cut strays loose with a dejected shake of the head and a mumbled, "Gawd knows, I tried!"

The concept of family has pretty well gone down the pike. It's hard to find a family where the mama and the daddy and the aunts and uncles and the grandparents and great-aunts and -uncles are still together at times other than holidays. How often on a nothing night in October do you find the family gathered in a modern household? It's hard to perpetuate the concept of Christian family when its antecedent is virtually unknown.

Even if I wrote run-on sentences longer than St. Paul's I wouldn't achieve his diverse distribution or his literary longevity, but I think I am going to win in the long run. Tell me, Sir, did you have your babies around long enough to get carrots on your new white toga? Well, that's too bad. You lose.

5

THOMAS CARLISLE SPENT EIGHTEEN YEARS WRIT-
ING HIS FIRST GREAT LITERARY WORK AND THE
HOUSEKEEPER BURNED IT IN THE FIREPLACE. HE
WAS A SLOPS AND HAD LEFT IT ALL OVER THE FLOOR.
SHE SAID IT WAS AN ACCIDENT BUT I SUSPECT SHE HAD
READ THE BOOK. HE WROTE IT AGAIN FROM MEMORY.

If this column goes in the Thursday trash we will have
a transcribed interlude of organ music this month, because
I can't seem to remember anything more demanding than
my phone number.

That Carlisle gem comes from my almost limitless
collection of irrelevant facts. Since they are apropos of nothing at all, I can remember them forever. They gather dust
on the unused shelf most of the time for obvious reasons.
Try working into a conversation the fact that half of all mon-
keys are left-handed or that the uniforms of the Light Brigade were cherry red and baby blue. People look at you
funny. I resort to it today in sheer desperation.

I ought always to write my November column before I deliver my annual autumnal temper tantrum on the
deplorable state of education almost everywhere. It is my
usual Parents Night fare. We always have a fine turnout, which
is very gratifying, but I noticed this year that although 375
people were mashed into the church, the two rows immediately in front of me were vacant. They were probably afraid
of powder burns. When I am through with that diatribe I
have exhausted both the issues and my ire for weeks. It's
like Will Cuppy said about the Pharaoh Cheops, "He built
the Great Pyramid — and then he felt better."

From my surveys this year I find that there are a growing number of economically distressed schools and they are just about distressed enough to give up on chili suppers and rummage sales and opt for black jack and roulette. The state of the economy, and a little help from planned parenthood, have many of us right around the jugular. Tuition, along with everything else, went up. Enrollment went down. In searching for answers to my particular situation I found a string of replies that sounded very much like this. "A few years ago we thought private school was important for our children, so we took an extra job to pay for it. It's still important and we are still working, but now we can't afford it." I understand that perfectly, but understanding it, I still cannot remedy it. If someone tells me they don't think I have the finest music program extant, or that my car pool lines are in a constant state of collapse, or that instead of teaching Spanish we perhaps ought to teach Tibetan, and if we follow their sage advice they might enroll, I can control that. I may not change a thing, but I could.

I don't see anything I can do about this economic crunch. I'm sorry I don't know, but I'm not surprised. As a kindergartner pointed out to me in a testing session last week when I asked him what day came after Tuesday, "I'm new in this school and I can't be expected to know everything." I can't be expected to know what to do about the economy, but what really frightens me is that it begins to appear that nobody else knows either. From whence cometh the cavalry?

How does one survive an inflated depression with a tittle on the end? I did not get my solution from Adam Smith or even Milton Friedman. I got it from Sophie Tucker. The occasion was the reopening of the old Balinese Room after a fire in the fifties. Sophie Tucker was the major attraction. She was being interviewed concerning her book, *One of These Days*. It recounted all her trauma from the time she was smuggled out of Russia in an oxcart, through her several marriages, to the state of success which allowed her to contribute over $4 million to Israel. The question was, "How did you survive all those early hardships?"

The answer was a succinct, "I just kept breathing." I plan to try.

6

WHAT IS A SCHOOLMARM TO DO? THE COUNTRY IS CELEBRATING THE 200TH YEAR OF THE CONSTITUTION — A DOCUMENT THAT REMAINS UNPARALLELED FOR INVENTIVE THOUGHT, CONSTRUCTIVE COMPROMISE AND UNRELENTING OPTIMISM IN THE ABILITY OF MANKIND TO GOVERN ITSELF FOR THE BENEFIT OF ALL AND THE ENRICHMENT OF NO PARTICULAR GROUP.

It's a time when schoolchildren should bask in the bounty of our forefather's forethought. I want mine to relish it and know that it is their responsibility to carry forth their heritage. I want that, but I'm a little abashed when it comes to teaching it. We've muddled through so far, but frankly, I'm darned if I know how.

The morning paper is a case in point. The Congress of the United States is interviewing Judge Bork to see if he is worthy of their consent to serve on the Supreme Court of the United States. They've been preening before the cameras for some days now. The head of the committee is impeached by the press for plagiarism — and it would appear that the press has a pretty good case. Also on the committee are a couple of senators who bumble when you ask them their names. There is another very vocal one who ran into a little difficulty with a situation we refer to as "Chappaquiddick." Are these our best offering to our children as paragons of virtue equipped to govern the country?

If you are working days and can't watch the tube, but you were on vacation during the summer and watched daytime, what did you get? You got the Contra hearings, ad nauseam. And what did they show you? How about a good-looking Marine with whom we all fell in love until morning light when we thought about folks taking the fate of our country into their own individual hands. Then specters of Aaron Burr and John Brown and John Wilkes Booth rose to haunt us. They did, that is, if we were educated before the recent revamping of history by the textbook companies, and we still knew who Aaron Burr and John Brown and John Wilkes Booth were.

Some twenty-five years ago a gentleman of sand-hill renown was walking through the bank lobby and a local banker began to rag him. "Mr. Pete," he called loudly so everybody in the bank could hear. "Lyndon just called and wants you to come to Washington and help him run the country."

Without even slowing his gait, Mr. Elder replied, "There was a time when I could have done that but the mule-eared ____ ____ ____ has it so messed up now, even I can't straighten it out."

I'm with you, Mr. Elder. I'm not sure how I can teach it so that the generation I'm responsible for is going to know just what it is that's worth their effort to preserve, protect and defend.

Our forefathers prayed for guidance before every session of the Constitutional Convention in Philadelphia in 1787. It seemed to pull them through. I suppose our best course of action is to rely on the same intervention now. Let us pray.

7

THERE ARE SOME THINGS THAT ARE CONSIDERED GENERALLY NECESSARY TO SALVATION IN EPISCOPAL SCHOOLS AND PLANNING A PRODUCTION FOR CHRISTMAS IS ONE OF THEM. THESE COME IN DIFFERENT SHAPES AND SIZES AND SERVE PURPOSES OTHER THAN THE SIMPLE COMMEMORATION OF CHRISTMAS.

Politics often runs rampant in a discreet sort of way. My first grade does the pageant part and I have watched some mothers begin back in pre-kindergarten running their daughter for Virgin Mary.

When this true-spirit-of-Christmas began to disrupt the orderly transfer of knowledge almost a month before it should have, I decided, with Solomon-like wisdom, to solve the problem by drawing names for the principal parts. I have been doing that for six years and it is amazing how many mothers — parents of the unchosen, of course — still do not believe this is the selection process. The King of France used to have to be born in public so the people would be sure there had not been a change. I am thinking of hiring a hall for the drawing this year myself.

This process has backfired on me on other occasions also. I didn't promise you it was foolproof. Several years ago I had duly chosen the principals. The remainder were angels and animals. We had arrived at dress rehearsal and I was doing my headmistress bit getting the red socks off the angels and the bubble gum away from Melchior and Caspar when the real crisis occurred. Joseph opted out.

Taking Joseph by the arm gently so as not to leave bruises, we went outside to talk it over. It finally boiled down

21

to me saying between clenched teeth, "But why don't you want to be Joseph? Joseph is a very good part." And he, with tears rolling his cheeks, sobbed, "Yeah, but the cows have the best suits."

In the event that you think my experience is limited to one county fair and a turkey shoot, let me hasten to assure you that I have done Christmas programs on three continents. I once taught fifth grade at the American Elementary School in Mannheim, Germany. It was a mammoth establishment boasting six sections of each grade, a P.E. teacher, dance instructor, reading specialist, speech coach, and two — count 'em — two music teachers. Right away you can see an Xmas production shaping up that, in size and scope, will rival *Oliver*. To sweeten the pot, both music teachers were dating the speech coach and were intent on impressing him for reasons that continue to elude me.

Everybody participated. I was given a role commensurate with my talent and ability. I pulled the curtain. After exhibiting great timing and dexterity in this feat, I was rewarded with a padding of my part. I also snowed on the villagers.

If practice makes perfect we should have hit Broadway about mid-November because sometimes I was called out of class to snow on the villagers five and six times a day. After each successful snowstorm, I would sweep up the Styrofoam particles, lower the line containing the paper bags with appropriate holes, and replace my slightly shopworn snow. Besides being wearing on the disposition, it was a trifle hard on the cotton clothesline which held the snow bags. Nonetheless, with dogged determination, I persevered.

We opened on December 21, 1958. We were magnificent. We were, that is, through my initial snowing on the villagers. I then pulled the curtain for their entrance into the village church and watched in frozen horror as my battle-fatigued snow bag line was rent in twain from the top to the bottom. It arced in a perfect parabola, picking up the Baby

Jesus from the creche and flinging him into the amazed arms of the Commanding General in the third row.

I left for a Christmas Pilgrimage to the Holy Land the following morning. It was not a moment too soon.

8

EPIPHANY IS THAT SEASON OF THE YEAR WHEN THE WISEMEN HAVE COME AND GONE AND YOU HAVE TO START WRITING YOUR OWN CHAPEL LECTURES AGAIN. CHRISTMAS IS A HARD ACT TO FOLLOW. I LOOK FORWARD WITH GREAT GLEE TO GIVING UP CHAPEL LECTURES FOR LENT. IN THE MEANTIME I SEARCH FOR A SIX-PART THEME.

There are just lots of dandy stories I could choose from. The Bible is full of tantalizing tales, but I've been at this a long time and I've already used up most things with six convenient parts. The Judges of Israel kept the little angels on the edge of their seats. And why not? They relate to things like Sampson setting fire to foxes and running them through a cornfield. It's prime time television fare.

I decided to range a little farther afield and give the Philistines equal time. Haven't you always wondered what a Philistine did on Saturday? Apparently neither have my students because they listened politely, and then rather pointedly asked what King David was doing all this time.

I'll tell you what King David was doing. He was trying to get his kids to behave. Poor old King David just had it up the getis with those kids. There was Absalom holding a sit-in at the gates of Jerusalem proclaiming to all comers that he could dispense justice better than old Dad. There was ambitious, manipulating Adonijah, none too short on self-esteem, putting old Dad in a box by blatantly proclaiming that he was King. And then there was Solomon. If David had anything at all to be thankful for, it was that Solomon didn't have a BankAmericard. He bankrupted his kingdom by over-extending his resources, expanding the bureaucracy and over-spending his funds, but without the plastic it took him longer. I can see him now, charging Tyre. And why didn't the mighty king of Israel put a stop to it? The writer of Kings states it rather succinctly: "David had never at any time displeased his sons by asking, 'Why have you done thus and so?'"

We are terribly hung-up these days on child abuse, and there is certainly none among us who is going to advocate it, but an occasional bust on the backside to alter the course of childhood cannot be equated with abuse. Anyone who has had occasion to share time in close quarters with a three-year-old knows that they are by nature tyrannical. Sometimes they grow out of it. Sometimes they are reasoned out of it. But most often they should be jerked out of it. Not to do so because it displeases the child borders on either cowardice or lunacy. Civilization is the ability to live in some semblance of peace in a community. That is a learned trait, and what is learned has to be taught by somebody or some set of circumstances. Yet some parents believe that to teach a child deprives him of the right to be master of his fate. I have a one word answer for that. Two syllables.

I daily watch parents being tyrannized by their children because they don't want to do anything to displease them. And very often when problems arise at school or the playing fields they are unable to relate this to their own lack of guidance. How can the poor baby do what's acceptable when nobody ever told him forcefully what was? It takes a lot of love to discipline your own child, and a lot of time.

Teddy Roosevelt once was hearing a recital of the willful antics of his now legendary daughter, Alice Roosevelt Longworth. His oft-quoted comment was, "I can control Alice or run the country, but I can't do both."

A good many of us are faced with the same choice. We find it much easier to confront a striking union, whom we don't particularly love, than to confront and displease an obstreperous child whom we do. David just made the easier choice. And you see what he got for it.

9

REVISIONISTS HAVE BEEN MESSING AROUND WITH HISTORICAL FACT FOR YEARS NOW, AND I'VE BEEN KICKING SAND AND MUTTERING, BUT THIS IS TOO MUCH. NOW THEY'VE GONE AND DONE IT WITH THE ALAMO.

I've been at the Alamo regularly since I was a toddler. It's a part of my heritage. Then it became part of my shortcut from the Medical Arts Building where my orthodontist had his shop to the Menger Hotel Coffee Shop where I consoled myself with a little pain-killing-health-giving chess pie. I did a lot of business around the Alamo and I don't want anybody monkeying around with it. I'm a Daughter of the Republic and we are there to protect it.

In the fifties when John Wayne became Davy Crockett and Richard Widmark became Jim Bowie, I became a real Alamo junkie. Remember the opening scene of the show? Wide screen. Lonesome cowboy on vast expanse of land singing, "The Ballad of the Alamo"? I must have seen the show a couple of dozen times, and I know it's factual because in all that time they never once changed their testimony.

The John Wayne version came out when I was a young teacher. I took my whole class to see it. I used to do that sort of thing frequently. If there was something I wanted to do and couldn't work it into my already overcrowded schedule, I just took the whole class and called it a field trip. The event was always something like a movie, or the circus, so the kids liked it, and I called it educational. You could get by with that sort of stuff then. Dewey was still around and we all learned to pronounce "experiential education" on our way to the movie.

Sitting on the barricade of the Alamo, watching Santa Anna on his white horse with his beautiful army coming slowly toward you and blowing that daunting bugle is a spine-tingling experience. Dewey would have loved it.

Tonight NBC showed a remake of *The Alamo.* I watched it all the way through. It was okay. Not great, you understand, but okay. Jim Arness is about as close to John Wayne as one can come, so of course they didn't have him playing the John Wayne/Davy Crockett part. Some carpet-bagger cast him as Jim Bowie/Richard Widmark. This Davy Crockett didn't wear a coonskin cap or carry his long rifle that still resides at the Alamo. It was almost subversive.

Travis was a very sympathetic character. I remember when he was stiff-necked and arrogant. Can't imagine what miracle changed him. Fannin came off pretty poorly, but I don't care. I never liked Fannin anyway. What was really wrong with the whole production was that they didn't play "The Green Leaves of Summer." I can get misty-eyed over "The Green Leaves of Summer" going between the grocery store and the self-service filling station. A whole generation of our youth is going to grow up dry-eyed and deprived over this omission.

It might be that the NBC version is more accurate than the movie, but somehow I doubt it. Besides, accurate versions of history are often deadly dull, lacking verve, and swash and buckle. This one buckled a little bit.

I taught Texas History to a whole generation of our youth. When I retired from the classroom I taught the next teacher to teach it. Often I suited up again for one more farewell performance in the Texas History saga. Sarah Bernhardt ate her heart out. My rendition relied rather heavily on the Gospel According to John Wayne.

I was perpetuating a legend, I knew, but I really hadn't signed on to perpetuate a myth. I got all the main facts right. Santa Anna did capture the Alamo in thirteen

27

days and there weren't a whale of a lot of folk left to tell how it happened. If I had signed on knowingly for mythology, I would have the brave Texians soundly thrash Santa Anna at the Alamo, then follow him to Gonzales where once again he would learn not to mess with Texas and we would have avoided the unpleasantness of the Runaway Scrape in its entirety. I'd still keep San Jacinto. I like that part.

NBC's version was not without merit. Santa Anna still rode a white horse and all the notes on the *deguello* were the same, but whoever heard of not playing "The Green Leaves of Summer?" Bummer.

Here's something frightening to contemplate. If I lived long enough and taught long enough and was allowed to range free, unfettered by fact, I could change history in one generation. I could have it anyway I wanted it. Are you sure history is not being bent to suit the whims of the teacher, or the textbook publisher, or the TV producer right now in classrooms throughout the land? Think on it. We all argue until our dying day that the version we heard as children is the correct one. You need to make sure what that version is. Just to be on the safe side, maybe you better teach your children your family lore yourself.

Ready everybody? Key of C. "The Green Leaves of Summer are calling me home. . ."

10

IT'S LATE AFTERNOON. THIS DIGITAL THINGUS THAT SOMETIMES GIVES THE CORRECT TIME IS FLASHING THE GO-HOME HOUR. I'VE BEEN WORKING ON THE BUDGET AND RELATED UNPLEASANT ITEMS ALL DAY. I'M SO TIRED I DON'T KNOW WHETHER I'M AFOOT OR ON HORSEBACK.

Usually before I leave my desk I make a list of all those things that I have left undone that I ought to have done in the hope that they will reach miraculous completion on the morrow. It rarely happens, but I have grown accomplished at list-making. In a fit of downright contrariness I have decided that today I will make a list of all the things I am *not* going to do tomorrow.

1. Tomorrow I shall refuse to become exercised over the rotten state of education in the United States of America and all its foreign possessions. Pretty soon the dust is going to settle and the folk who want their children educated will see to it that they get educated. All those who are trying to make silk purses out of sow's ears will turn to another project. America didn't have universal public education when the Declaration of Independence and the Constitution were written, but the Founding Fathers managed to spell all of the words right. Two hundred years later we haven't changed many of them. I shall not worry about it.

2. The breakup of AT&T does not possess the same degree of magnitude as, say, dropping the atomic bomb on Hiroshima, even though I think it is getting the same amount of publicity. I expect I will be able to find a telephone that works somewhere for less money than it takes to go to

Europe. When my equipment dies I'll look around. Today I feel that if my telephone never rang again it would be a sign of God's blessing. I'm not going to worry about it.

3. Martin Luther King's birthday was a recent news-making event. I have no objection to his pep squad spelling it out for Martin, but it does make one wonder what the Congress of the United States was thinking about when they ignored the contributions of Thomas Jefferson, Benjamin Franklin and George Mason, designating no day in honor of them, and proceeded to make Martin Luther King's birthday a holiday. On the other hand, it doesn't make one wonder. Years divisible by four have a dulling effect on reason. Staunchly, I refuse to worry about it.

4. I shall not lose sleep over Pennzoil's case of pique with Texaco for dancing with Getty. I'm sure they will all come to some creative and mutually lucrative settlement and I shall discover it at the pumps.

5. Not the ERA, the IRA, the CIA or the IRS. You're on your own, boys. I refuse to give you a thought.

6. I shall spend no time whatever on the Shiites and the Druse. Sometimes their mamas can't even tell the Druse from the Shiites. All I know for sure is that throughout my lifetime the reports from that part of the world will be the same. You can count on it. It's been happening since about page five of the Bible. The stars change but the script's the same. Once we called them Hittites and Philistines and another time Sumerians and Assyrians and even again Babylonians, but like a Barbara Courtland novel, the plot is predictable. I can't change it and I refuse to worry about it tomorrow or the next day.

This morning in chapel I was sitting with the four-year-olds, as is my custom. I usually have a different one on my lap daily but recently I found Emily there more often than her rotation would warrant. Emily was sitting fairly quietly through the reading of the lessons. Isaiah ain't for everyone,

30

and Emily had done her best to follow the story line.

"Miss Hollamon," she croaked in a resounding whisper. "Why doesn't he show the pictures when he reads?"

Now there is something for a headmistress to worry about. I promise, Emily, to put that on my calendar and give it my full attention in the morning. Life looks better when you take care of the important things first.

11

DUE TO LACK OF INSPIRATION THIS MONTH, THE "HICKORY STICK" HAS BEEN CANCELED. PERHAPS NOT ENTIRELY CANCELED, JUST ABBREVIATED.

If you're waiting for me to tell you why I am being less lippy this month, I will submit this much. I have ceased and desisted from saying that things were going to get better. I made that mistake in January. I said, "Cheer up, things could be worse." I did, and they were.

The Plagues of Egypt have looked like the Senior Guild's silver tea compared to life in Galveston recently. And the only lesson I can glean from watching this is that a substance more powerful than Super Glue is the expectation of excellence. Those folks from whom excellence is expected make it. Those from whom it is not demanded, crash.

How long has it been since we said to kids, "It's not what happens to you; it's how you handle it that counts"? How long has it been since we said flatly to a child, "You are expected to handle that situation adroitly because that is the kind of background you come from. Ergo, you will." We haven't overdone that act because (a) not everybody comes from the same background and we do not wish to discriminate, and (b) the message forced upon us with the regulations from agencies admonishes us that our mission is to teach school, not build character.

The old McGuffey reader was reprinted recently as a period piece and I read a copy. Every story in it stressed character-building. I like to put that in juxtaposition with a story I once found in a basal reading series I read when I taught fifth grade back in '02. It was concerning the

"Wonderful Cornfield" in which Paracutin arose. There was a passage stating that if Juan didn't want to farm there, the government would give him another piece of land in exchange. I skipped that story every year. The lesson learned was that the government giveth and the government taketh away, rather than there was a volcano there. I probably overreacted. Kids probably didn't learn either one.

Today we hear a constant cry to get back to the basics. When one is being held at gunpoint, or has just been severely beaten and robbed, the nature of basics changes rather rapidly. The emphasis shifts from the syntax of sentences and the spelling of chrysanthemum to whether, in fact, anybody has ever taught you to simply hang in. Sometimes we call it moral development. Sometimes we call it survival. In either case, with the world we have to live in, we had better consider this an integral part of our curriculum. Because, if we do not teach our students the expectation of excellence, we really teach them nothing at all.

12

THEY CALL IT THE YEAR OF THE CHILD. CYNICAL LAUGHTER IS UNBECOMING A HEADMISTRESS; NONETHELESS, WE TOLERATE IT IN THOSE OF US FOR WHOM THE YEAR OF THE CHILD HAS STRETCHED TO TWENTY. AS A FORMER COLLEGE TOUR DIRECTOR, I THINK I SHALL ENTITLE MY TREATISE, "THE YEAR OF THE CHILD AND ITS ENVIRONS."

We have just extolled the Year of the Child by honoring his grandparents. Kids shaped up beautifully for that one. They sang magnificently, were scholastically impeccable, and resisted the impulse to shoot paper clips across rooms while their grandparents were watching — a feat of self-control unprecedented in school memory. Grandparents thought we had perfect control. We were careful not to leave bruises.

Grandparents Day is unabashedly designed to correlate with the annual fund drive. They threw people like me out of the Temple, but not, I notice, before we had made the sale. Grandparents Day is a marvelous occasion for beginning the soft sell. How else can one so blatantly display their wares? And in piling one's accomplishments up for display, one provides an excellent vehicle for taking stock.

I suspect that when you start recounting Mini-mester offerings in subjects such as photography, archaeology, cooking and the free enterprise system you will find that enrichment activities are well represented in Episcopal schools. The teaching of government and history through trips to Washington and around Texas isn't really too shabby a way to learn. It will never replace multiplication tables, but it makes the rest of the medicine go down rather easily. McGuffey isn't in any grave danger but boredom may be.

It is in the preparation of these showings, regardless of how ulterior the motive, that one pulls together what we used to call in survey courses "An Overview of Our Educational System." With a title like that it's no wonder it never sold a dozen copies. A word of warning, however — when preparing a dog and pony show of this flavor, prepare carefully. It is better to plop the carousel of slides on "Life at Trinity School" on the projector than to grab the art teacher's thesis slides on "Nudes in 20th Century Painting" and show five slides before diving hysterically at the projector. I'm still in a state of shock.

I'm rambling incoherently but my point is a simple one. For Episcopal schools to offer the caliber education we do for the price we do is truly to perform a service, and if in showing off we manage to raise a couple of lousy inflated dollars in order to continue the service, it's not a mortal sin. We're doing it for children — and isn't this the Year of the Child?

13

THE DIN AND ROAR YOU CAN PROBABLY HEAR ALL THE WAY TO YOUR HOUSE IS LITTLE OLYMPICS PRACTICE. I WAS JUST THERE. I WENT TO SURVEY MY DOMAIN TO ASCERTAIN WHAT TYPE OF REVOLUTION MUST BE TAKING PLACE IN THE HINTERLANDS TO RAISE SUCH A RUCKUS. I WAS GREETED BY A SHINING UP-TURNED FACE CLUTCHING A STOPWATCH WHO AN-NOUNCED PROUDLY, "I'M KEEPING TIME."

What a marvelous statement to make. I don't seem to be able to keep any of it at all. I never was any great shakes at holding on to money, but I can even do better at that than I can conserving time. I knew I was in bad trouble when I began making my list of things to do today and it ran off the bottom of my Big Chief tablet. Usually my list contains a few items that are designed to be postponed like (1) call the Feds and explain how to curb inflation, and (2) stamp out poverty in India. Recently I haven't encumbered myself with postponables.

I read this great book written by a man in a big paneled office with three secretaries. He said to set priorities. Don't shackle yourself with counting paper clips. I can't even find the paper clips. Delegate authority, he said. He didn't say to whom.

For the average Episcopal school administrator, this time of year is a horror show. The list of alternatives from which we choose is fascinating. It reads a lot like those choices in well-known personality inventories where they ask whether you had rather build a boat or conduct a symphony. "None of the above" is not a choice.

Would you rather: (a) Iron so you won't wear rumpled clothes to school or finish the grant proposal? (b) Get gas in old Green so you won't hike to school or revamp a horrendous Honors Day program? (c) Plan the Commencement program or get out the Fund Drive material? Not one of your choices is (d) Go to Hawaii for a week or choose the Green House if you prefer.

One thing we did choose. We chose to cast our lot with Episcopal education, and I suspect that if they resurrected the Inquisition and planned a little auto-da-fe in our honor, not one of us would recant this choice. The month of May just goes with the territory, and all the September planning in the world is not going to alter half a line.

May has one great attribute. It's followed by June when we can "keep time," and count the victories. In the meantime, we bought it, Babe.

My immediate choice is whether to finish this frazzling column, which nobody probably reads anyway, or cut my losses and go to the gym for a course in remedial fat called, in the vernacular, Aerobic Dancing. "Oh World, thou choosest not the better part . . ."

14

I CALL MYSELF BEING ON VACATION. IT IS A CONCEPT THAT HAS APPARENTLY NOT ACHIEVED UNIVERSAL ACCEPTANCE. SINCE I AM ALREADY DOING PENANCE BEING CHAINED TO THIS FRAZZLING DESK, I DETERMINED TO GO "TODAS PORKUS" AND BEGIN ON THE CHAPEL LECTURES FOR NEXT FALL. LORD KNOWS, THAT'S PENANCE.

Yearly, I've tried to sidestep the issue with the grace and agility of Markova. I have spoken on the Wonders of the Ancient World and Comparative Religions. I have enraptured them with Lost Civilizations. Von Daniken ate his heart out. But somehow the Bible always kept worming its way into the act.

It's not that the Bible is new on the Bestseller List for me. I can rattle off verses with the facility of nursery rhymes. At the great University of Hook 'Em I had a Bible course every semester — for reasons I need not explain to those who frequented that bastion of learning in the early fifties. It has toughened up considerably since then.

In point of fact, I can make much more sense out of nursery rhymes than I can out of parts of the Bible. Nursery rhymes are political satire. The Old woman Who Lived in the Shoe referred to Queen Anne and her multitudinous brood. Jack Horner was the Abbot of Glastonbury during the reign of Henry VIII and Mary Quite Contrary was Mary, Queen of Scots. I have it on the best authority. Those facts are not too much of a hill for the unexpanded pragmatic mind to climb, but every year I live in fear that some kid will ask me about the parables. You see, nobody ever read me

Chapter Two on parables, and there never was a sixth grader who didn't ask "What if?" about everything.

For example:

1. If the prodigal son got his full share early on and blew it, whose calf got barbecued? Is that fair?

2. If everybody gets paid the same whether they work in the vineyard eight hours or eight minutes, how many folks are going to show up for the early shift on day two? Isn't it important to work hard?

3. If the servant who buried his talent and was reprimanded for it had instead invested in fertilizer tanks in West Texas when it appeared to be a flourishing business, what would have happened? Shouldn't one be extremely careful with other people's money?

He might have missed the whole point, but are you going to not answer his question? *Can* you answer his question? When we do parables I plan to have an extended case of the chicken pox.

It is not my intent to be flip about the Bible. The point I wish to make is that most of us are acceptably prepared in academic pedagogy. I am not that confident about our religious pedagogy. We teach in Christian schools. Shouldn't we be equally well prepared?

That answer doesn't have to be reasoned in Socratic syllogism, but try this one. How are we going to get that way short of seminary? There was a Bethel Bible Class offered here that appeared made to order; however, it required nine hours a week of study. I don't spend nine hours a week sleeping. I think the answer may lie in in-service workshops at the SAES and NAES conferences. As president of the Southwest Association of Episcopal Schools, I would be most happy for us to sponsor something like that, but when it is presented I fervently pray that it does not consist solely of three choruses of "Jesus Wants Me for a Sunbeam." I am interested in how to handle Chapter Two.

15

WE ARE OPEN FOR BUSINESS, FULL UP, AND FUNC-
TIONING. THAT MAY SOUND LIKE A TRIVIAL
STATEMENT FOR A HEADMISTRESS TO MAKE IN
SEPTEMBER BUT IT DOES NOT COME EASILY TO THE
TONGUE. BY THIS TIME OF YEAR WE ARE EITHER SMIL-
ING AND SERENE OR COMATOSE AND INCOMMUNICADO.
I USUALLY FALL INTO THE SECOND CATEGORY.

I always pray for moderate rains and showers on
opening day for superstitious reasons. This time I got something that made the Rains of Ranchipur look like morning
dew. Three hundred little bodies pushed and shoved each
other in the hall. There weren't enough big book covers,
McGraw-Hill sent the wrong Spanish books, and coffee was
late for the opening day parents' meeting.

I got only the new parents in the tent for parents'
meeting anyway. The old hands had already had boat drill
and knew about abandoning ship before they got put on
clean-up committee for the Blessing of the Pets.

In any case, the tumult and shouting have died and
it is time to contemplate the next move. I have always treated
the old adage about fool's names and fool's faces with the
contempt it deserved. That attitude presents opportunities
to fan it around the country being area-wide Big Mouth and
speaking on a variety of subjects. I used to have one autumnal temper tantrum about the state of education and let it
go at that. Now it's Dial-a-Tantrum. The possibilities are unlimited. Try this one.

The *Wall Street Journal* had an article in their September 5th issue, front page, which stated: SCHOOL HISTORY

BOOKS STRIVING TO PLEASE ALL. MARKET FACTORS OUTWEIGH QUEST FOR TRUTH. Now there is a built-in tantrum worthy of a volume instead of a column. History ignoring truth! Scott Foresman dumped $500,000 into this new series called *America! America!* and they merry well expect it to sell. To that end they have included black cowboys, woman pirates, Haight Ashbury hippies, an Indian boy, a Chicano grandmother, and a middle-aged Oriental. The only thing I didn't locate was a one-eyed female P.O.W. I'm sure they will correct that in the next edition. What they have not included are facts. The publishers claim a "limited listing of facts" and extol the "variety exemplifying the pluralism of America." To those not fluent in educationese, that's the woman pirate/hippie part.

Can you believe we have arrived at a state of grace where history shouldn't be colored by fact? No textbook publisher should be allowed that right. This book pretends, for instance, that the Civil War solved the problem of race relations in this country. I hope the people in Los Angeles and Detroit, circa 1965, see that part.

But surely this insanity has not permeated the actual classrooms, you say? Guess again, Sport. *America! America!* is one of the biggest sellers on the eight-grade market today. It sells for about $10 a copy. It came out in September 1977 and sold 67,000 copies last year. They plan a major revision in two years. I guess they figure they can make up something new by then.

How long, oh Lord? First we allowed textbook folk to foist modern math on us, thereby supplying ourselves with a generation of folk conversant with Boolean algebra but inept at long division. Then we rearranged the English language allowing no rules on syntax to prevail for fear of hurting someone's feelings. Now we take away historical fact and substitute "pluralism." It is incredible in the truest sense of the word.

There are 110,000 students in Episcopal schools in

this country taught by 9,000 teachers. If our education provides them with anything, let it be the security of parameters in this world and the comfort of an absolute.

Quite obviously we are going to have to do it without the aid of textbook publishers. We may have to create our own textbooks. I think I'll get started immediately on mine and this time I think I'll let the South win.

16

POLISH STUDENTS WANT FREE TIME, AND THE UAW WANTS FRINGE BENEFITS. I AM ACQUAINTED WITH BOTH. ONE OF THE FRINGE BENEFITS OF WHAT WE CALL "MATURITY" IS A TAD OF FREE TIME BETWEEN THREE AND FOUR A.M. WE CALL IT THE THREE O'CLOCK WAKE-UPS. LIKE THE KU KLUX KLAN, FEW DIVULGE THEIR MEMBERSHIP UNTIL CONFRONTED WITH A FELLOW TRAVELER.

One is not a full-fledged member if he has joined as a result of a superb dinner after which his host insists he have a liqueur. He knew full well what would happen. He brought it on himself, and I hope he spent the waking hours calculating his income tax. Full-fledged members are those who wake up after having a judicious dinner, their vitamin pills, taking their exercises, and saying their prayers. In a more gracious age they would have been called the undeserving poor.

This time does not have to be a tossing, turning waste, I kept telling myself. One can plan, dream and indulge in flights of fancy. You will notice that I did not say fantasize. That has a different connotation these days. I'm not knocking it. I'm just not discussing it.

I have always been good at flights of fancy. One of my better ones was having the lights dim in the theater, the music come up and the screen blast: "Budgie Hollamon Presents . . ." I got that from the Palace picture show where Sol Hurok presented. Later when I got grown and went to the big city, Edna W. Saunders presented. When I really learned hard things, like reading an airline schedule, I was also sophisticated enough to know that Sol Hurok and Edna W. Saunders did not own all those things they presented. They just made the arrangements to bring them to the public. A walk in the park, I said. Surely, I, too, can do these magnificent things.

During the course of everyone's career there is the opportunity to try your hand at a flight of fancy and, yea, verily, I got mine. I was sitting at a board meeting of Episcopal Schools when I was called to the phone. I was so delighted to learn that the school had not burned down, or the entire Island population been decimated by the Infectious Ugh that I heard myself accept with alacrity the opportunity to present to the City of Galveston the one — the almost only — the famous and much desired Magna Carta! I was even excited about it. That's called either ignorance or innocence. Pick the one you like a lot.

The one, the almost only, Magna Carta does not come free with a couple of box tops. The opening price is $3,000 per day. "Worth it," I said. "Cheap at twice the price," I said. Bite your tongue.

I came home and spent the evening on the phone trying to fade my munificent gesture. I was immediately successful due to the generosity of Galvestonians. Relieved, I heaved a sigh and began planning. I would have it in Eaton Hall with banners and shields and get the Beefeater costumes from British Airways and have madrigal music and pour champagne.

And then it was morning. The sun rose, and so did reality. Galveston is an island and, therefore, by definition unsafe for Magna Carta, I guess. In any case, I have to store it in Houston and pay portal-to-portal security. There's publicity and printing costs and professional movers to heist the thousand-pound case up and down the stairs. The medieval case in which it was to be exhibited never got built because the builders were otherwise occupied cleaning up after the Grand Hotel fire. The madrigal music is lost in the mail somewhere between Galveston and Austin. And Lord knows where the press kit resides. It is not in Galveston.

The Beefeater costumes are not for loan, and the Venerable Dean will not appear in his Venerable Dean Suit because he has to remain at the Lincoln Cathedral. My parade hath been rainéd on. Nonetheless, the Magna Carta will appear in Eaton Hall in all its pristine purity. All we can offer is pristine purity. The accouterments died. It will be open to the public at no admission in March. You are invited to see it.

When you come, shed a tear for my lost Grand Design. I could have been such a success with shields and banners and madrigal music and klieg lights slashing the sky. Enjoy it for me. I probably won't get to see it because I shall be running in ever-decreasing concentric circles trying to get the show on the road. Face it. I flunked impresario. I'm not even an entrepreneur. Next bout of the three o'clock wake-ups I'm just going to compose my grocery list. It's cheaper that way.

17

I N THE LATE 19TH CENTURY WHEN THE INDUSTRIAL REVOLUTION IN ENGLAND HAD IMPRESSED THE WORLD, AND THE BUSINESS OF STATE WAS KEEPING VICTORIA BUSIER AND BUSIER, THE QUEEN DECIDED TO HAVE A BIG FANCY WORLD'S FAIR.

Technically it was for the purpose of showing off the English achievements to the world, but you and I know better. The real purpose was to keep Prince Albert off the streets. Albert didn't have a lot of duties, and he was rather good at finding things to amuse himself, so Victoria thought she'd put him in charge of a huge project that took so much time it would keep him out of salons. (A salon is defined as a high-class saloon in which the lady gives you the drink free.)

Albert did this one up right. He decided to house it in a big glass house you could see from everywhere. Albert's mother had evidently not told him about people who live in glass houses. This big glass house was supposed to serve as an inspiration to everyone who viewed the wonders of the 19th century world. He called it the Crystal Palace.

Also living in 19th century London were a group of entertainers who had a knack for political satire. They called themselves Cockneys. They entertained on street corners and they sang a ditty about Albert's Crystal Palace that went, "You could always see the Crystal Palace — if it wasn't for the houses in between."

I keep humming that ditty as I read the bombastic reports of the Blue Ribbon Committee on Education. The Blue Ribbon Committee has approached education as if it just sprang full grown from the head of Zeus. True, education is in a rotten state in many parts of this country, but it didn't just get there, and it didn't get there by choice. For years the education community, overworked and underpaid as it was, did a creditable and sometimes outstanding job. After all, we produced the group of folk that are now standing in judgement of the system. Tell me, did Ross Perot graduate from Heidelberg? The Sorbonne? Odessa Permian? I don't know where.

I have not always surveyed education from the seat of the headmistress. I began life teaching fifth grade at Juan Seguin Elementary. That was before we all integrated. I had Hispanics. I had fifteen in September, forty at Christmas, and fifteen again in May. Migrant laborers. I also did my stint at Lizzie M. Burges Elementary in Seguin, where I learned to conjugate the verb "to be." I be, you be, he bes. I have served my time in the field. I left public education because it was painfully evident that the constraints the federal government was placing upon teachers made it impossible to teach in the manner that was traditional for public schools. I was extremely lucky to have such a delightful alternative; one in which I could do my own thing.

My own thing was not a whit different than we had been doing in public education from 1954-1970 except for the religious emphasis. The only difference was that now we had this glossy new dream — this brave new world — this Crystal Palace which we were going to achieve by the grace of God and Titles One through Twelve. It could work. It may still work, but it will take a good number of years, if not generations, and in the meantime the child that is missing those things held dear by those of us who remember them is your child. And you, we, they are not happy about it. I am not surprised, but the method the committee seeks for correction is not only inept, it is silly.

Let us take athletics. They take lots of time. Most of it isn't school time. The part that is would be devoted to underwater basket weaving that last period in the afternoon if the student was not a scholar. So you take away athletics and what have you got? You have a restless batch of non-scholars killing time. They don't want to be in school. The teachers are not ecstatic about having them there, and the solution is not to cut out football, but to have funneled them toward vocational training before football ever got to be an alternative.

Let's take teacher competency. How are you going to measure that other than by the product they produce? Will a test do it? If the university that produced the teacher is not intimidated by the myriad rights laws that bind them, and if the test they take is not biased by its unbias, you might, but find me one of each. And when you have smiled at all that you have reached the second generation of ignorance. The second generation is terminal.

I just had a thank-you note from a lovely young lady who comes from a family of university professors. She is a teacher and a graduate of a fine university. She said, "I want to thank you for inviting Tom and I to your luncheon." I wept. Where did we go wrong? We went wrong years ago when we said all English is acceptable English if it is in standard usage. We said that not to hurt feelings. Now we reap the benefit of that and the fault is not the teachers — who, God knows, tried. It is the fault of the system that demanded it. Let's decide what we want from education no matter whose feelings are hurt.

A couple of generations from now we may have a fine amalgamated populace who speak a language now unknown and unaccepted. It may not be a tragedy. After all, we do not now speak Elizabethan English. But we have to be willing to accept what we have legislated or unlegislate it. We are not at the Crystal Palace yet. "You could always see the Crystal Palace — if it wasn't for the houses in between." We may tear them down or live with them. Neither situation is ideal, but neither are all the fuss and feathers flying.

Whose fault is the state of education? It's yours and your legislators. When votes no longer count toward education you may again view the Crystal Palace. Not before.

The Eighties

I Did It My Way
Francis Albert Sinatra

May Fete on the garth
Carlota '48

1

WHAT EVER HAPPENED TO THOSE OPENING LINES THAT HELD YOU SPELLBOUND THROUGH THE WHOLE FIRST CHAPTER? "I DREAMED LAST NIGHT THAT I RETURNED TO MANDERLEY." NOW, THERE'S A SIMPLE DECLARATIVE SENTENCE OF NOTE. HOW ABOUT "CALL ME ISHMAEL"? I READ THE WHOLE BOOK TRYING TO DISCOVER WHAT KIND OF MOTHER WOULD TAG A KID ISHMAEL.

But in casting around for opening lines to steal, I believe the one that best suits my purposes is: "Now is the winter of our discontent . . ." My discontent seems to be covering the calendar right thoroughly recently. The causes may be multiple, but the one that leaps most readily to mind is that I'm on the Scarsdale. Dieting is probably beautifying for the soul and beneficial for the body, but its therapeutic value to the disposition is questionable. It gives me a personality about as lovable as a spreading adder. Dieting is faddish and chic to some but to me it's a humiliating reminder that things have gotten out of hand and drastic measures have to be taken.

Okay, World, I'm doing my bit. What do you have in mind for shaping yourself up? Take the Middle East. There's a worthy project. Americans have been held hostage for over 100 days because a former ruler came to this country for surgery. If the Iranian students didn't want the Shah to leave the country, why did they allow him to go? A world that sits still for the shattering of established international law can't be much of a threat when it comes to a country's internal affairs. Haul him off the plane and hold him hostage. But that's done now, World. How are you going to shape that up?

That brings us to the Afghanistan affair. Surely our reaction to that invasion will survive in the annals of absurdity forever. Whether the Russian invasion of Afghanistan is our affair is not up for debate here. We loudly made it our affair. And stepping forth with the roar of a tiger we proclaim that if those soldiers aren't sent home we won't run in their relay races next summer. I've seen better threats in the Pre-school play yard. Surely, World, you can handle things better than that.

Then there are Abscam and Brilab. Caught flat-footed with both hands in the cookie jar and sugar all over their faces, our noble statesmen, makers of policy and shining lights of nobility to the free world, do not claim they are innocent. They claim that the way they got caught wasn't fair. What are you going to do now, Congress?

All of this is reported in ponderous verbiage full of sound and fury and containing no clout. The pen may be mightier than the sword but it has apparently run out of ink. Your shot, News Media.

Perhaps headmistresses are hawkish by nature. When they haul that kid into my office for flinging water bombs in the cafeteria, he knows merry well somebody's going to come off second and, in the great confrontation between him and me, it's not very likely to be me.

The *Galveston News* reported this event over the weekend: An eighty-year-old woman asked for cookies at a gathering in Cuney Park and was told she could have only two. Enraged, she threw a cup of punch on the server who promptly clouted her with the punch ladle. That's shaping a situation up!

Now is the winter of our discontent made glorious summer by a punch ladle wielder. When you're on a diet almost anything seems to improve your lot.

2

THE OBJECT IS TO RETURN FROM VACATION RE-
FRESHED. BUT THEN HERDING FIFTY KIDS AND
SEVENTY-EIGHT PIECES OF LUGGAGE AROUND
EUROPE FOR A MONTH IS JUST NOT VERY REFRESHING.
IT SHOULDN'T COME AS A SURPRISE TO ME. I'VE BEEN
DRAGGING HOME FROM TOURS FOR TEN YEARS. I'VE
MADE MORE FAREWELL APPEARANCES THAN SARAH
BERNHARDT, BUT THE SIGHT OF MY DESK PILED HIP-
DEEP CINCHED IT. THIS IS DEFINITELY AND ABSOLUTELY
MY FINAL FAREWELL TOUR. PRUDENCE DICTATES THAT
ONE STAY CLOSE ENOUGH TO HOME TO OPEN THE MAIL
ON AT LEAST A WEEKLY BASIS.

The job of a headmistress is mainly janitorial. One
sweeps all the trash and clutter out of the way for teachers
so they will have time to teach, but it is devoutly to be hoped
that the debris one is clearing bears *some* relation to the
business of education. Just a shouting similarity will suffice.
Evidence to support that contention is not to be found on
my desk in August.

What I find on my desk are important papers that
require immediate attention. They come in official envelopes
marked Texas Education Agency and Texas Department of
Human Resources and Texas Employment Commission.
That's enough to strike terror in your heart right there, and
well it should; for their contents, if not properly answered,
could put Johnny and his McGuffey on the sidewalk in front
of a door marked CLOSED.

Conscience and responsibility dictate that schools
should be safe from pestilence, earthquake, fire and flood.

By stretching Christian charity one might even sanction bureaucratic meddling into the block count in the kindergarten or the number of shaded areas on the playground. After all, no competent administrator is going to come out strongly in favor of sunstroke, but for the Ph.D. with oakleaf cluster in bureaucratic claptrap I submit the following. It comes from Part 3 of Form C-1 of the Texas Employment Commission's "Status Report" which is now mandatory for all schools.

> #10. Did you employ four or more individuals in Texas on a day in twenty different calendar weeks during any calendar year since 1971? If "yes" show the ending date of the twentieth such week.

In the event that you are uncertain about your response to this type question they have thoughtfully supplied Form C-1A to accompany C-1. This is entitled "Texas Employment Commission Instructions for Preparation of Status Report, Form C-1." I quote this helpful classic in its entirety:

> Item 6 and 7, answer the questions and supply the information printed in each of these items.

The proposal from the Texas Education Agency, which arrived on July 20 when most schools are closed, required a rebuttal, if there was to be one, by August 2, when most schools continue to be closed. The proposal was that all non-public schools accredited by TEA be required to hire only teachers with Texas teaching certificates. This would eliminate a good portion of the talent available to non-public schools. Teachers should assuredly be competent in the area in which they are employed, but I thoroughly resent the implication that no state or individual other than the Texas Education Agency is qualified to judge that competence. Trinity School teaches Spanish at all levels from pre-kindergarten through sixth grade. For the primary school we employ a native of Mexico who took her degree at Escuela Nacional Para Maestras de Jardines de Niños in Mexico City. She is certified by the Secretaria de Education Pública, and further than that, I know what she's doing and how she's doing it. I am not convinced that Texas history and government would enhance her value to Trinity or her ability to teach Spanish in kindergarten. To imply that it would is sheer bureaucratic pomposity.

Please remember that all of this is not for the purpose of being allowed to dip your biscuit in the public gravy boat. It is required in order to secure the right to keep your biscuit *out* of the public gravy boat.

These procedures are not totally useless, however. From these exercises we obtain answers to several often-asked questions. How else could we so graphically illustrate the reason for the state of education in this country today, or get such marvelous insight into why fat little gray-headed headmistresses are often found babbling incoherently on street corners.

3

MARY B. ERSKINE ELEMENTARY SCHOOL STARTED OFF THE SAME WAY EVERY YEAR. FIRST DAY WE HAD TO WRITE A PARAGRAPH ABOUT WHAT WE HAD DONE THAT SUMMER. I WAS ALWAYS HARD-PRESSED TO COME UP WITH SOMETHING OF EDUCATIONAL VALUE. I HAD USUALLY SPENT MY SUMMER FLOATING DOWN THE GUADALUPE IN AN INNERTUBE AND/OR WATCHING GENE AUTRY AND FROG MILHOUSE MAKE THE WORLD SAFE FOR DEMOCRACY DOWN AT THE PALACE PICTURE SHOW. NEITHER WERE IN THE LEAGUE WITH CLIMBING THE EMPIRE STATE BUILDING OR DESCENDING THE GRAND CANYON.

That's how I began my career in creative writing. Some refer to it more simply as the years when I perfected the art of lying.

I wish I was in Mary B. Erskine this year. I'd dazzle them with my fancy footwork. In June and July I went to Exeter to attend the seminar on Advance Administrative Leadership which Harvard does for seasoned school heads. Then I came back to Trinity where I audited the course in theology called Summer Bible School. It's a toss-up where I learned the most exotic things.

Some would call this Exeter escapade my mid-life crisis. I find that a monumental misnomer. Mid-life, indeed. How many hundred-year-old women do you know slogging around being goal-oriented? Nonetheless, I do confess that I had a change of direction in mind. My first choice for renewal was a couple of weeks at the fat farm, but the Board wouldn't swing for that. They did, surprisingly, smile beatifically on my second suggestion, which was the Harvard bit. The price was about the same. It didn't sound too bad replacing a Texas summer with a New England one. Besides, it gave five hours advance credit. Visions of doctorates danced in my head. I'm beginning to get a thing about doctorates. You see, I have signed this contract to write a book with a child psychiatrist. It goes down hard to visualize a dust jacket which reads, "by George Willeford, M.D., and Budgie Hollamon, Girl Scout."

The educational fare was varied. I had Personal Skills, Communication, Governance, Financial Management, Educational Leadership, and Mixed Doubles. I think I did best in tennis. I know the rules for that. Governance was a different soaper every day. They were all case studies about how some headmaster had gotten into hot water. They read like the 1955 *McCall's*. "Life had not been easy for Cliff and Cissy Chennelwick since he took over the headmastership of St. Grottelsex. . . ." I loved it.

Then there was Financial Management where we learned to look at a financial statement and tell which schools were cash poor but not bankrupt and which had really bought it. Apparently schools only come in those two flavors.

Educational Leadership wasn't. It was taught by two Ph.D.'s from Harvard, one each male and female. They taught me that Durkheim, the founder of functional sociology, said that you cannot get rid of authority in the classroom. I have twenty-four teachers who did not found functional sociology, who knew the same thing for free. I learned that Dr. Gilligan had done her doctoral work proving the premise that boys and girls are different. I'm just going to let that one sit there. I started planning my winter wardrobe when it was pointed out that Cinderella should not be taught in pre-schools because it was sexist literature. Furthermore, the hidden curriculum was that rank had privilege and that this privilege would exert itself in the end. Now, *that* takes an inventive mind.

And speaking of inventive minds and exotic curriculum, we return to Trinity where the annual end-of-summer-Bible-School is in progress. By August, mamas are so eager to sweep kids out of the house that one could offer Safe Cracking and Convenience Store Hijacking and fill up. That is not, however, the curriculum offered at Trinity. You may recall the paperback novels concerning the Q Document and the R Document. Our Bible School curriculum must be based on the M Document. M as in Mount. Carol Mount, to be precise. She is in charge of the cooking phase of this theological endeavor. On Monday she sent down the remains of the lesson on that great parable of the loaves and the cheese. Loaves and the *cheese*, Carol? Certainly. We can't have kids cutting up fish all over the Randall Center. The text is from "Parables for Vegetarians."

On Tuesday, we progressed to the 161st Psalm, which is reported to begin, *Butterflies are free domine*. Naturally, that brought forth butterfly cupcakes. On Wednesday we reached the apex. Wednesday's lesson came from that portion of the scripture where Jesus gathered the little children unto Him and taught them how to decorate sugar cookies.

How's that for a hidden curriculum? It's enough to give Harvard heartburn. Somehow, I feel better about my unadorned childhood. In fact, I think I'll raise a glass to Frog Milhouse.

4

I F OCTOBER IS THE MONTH OF GHOSTS AND GOB-
LINS, JULY IS THE MONTH OF KOOKS. I DO NOT EN-
TER INTO THIS DECISION LIGHTLY OR ILL-ADVISEDLY.
I SPEAK FROM EXPERIENCE. I WAS CAUGHT AT MY OF-
FICE IN JULY OPENING THE MAIL WHEN, ACCORDING TO
GOD AND HOYLE, I SHOULD HAVE BEEN OUT OF TOWN.
THE FOLLOWING OCCURRED:

A lady marched into my office unannounced followed
by a passel of kinder reminiscent of the Ringling Brothers'
Car Act. We sailed the uncharted waters of enrolling her
entire get in my school and beached on the shoals of tuition
costs. Carefully I explained that all monies paid to the school
were non-refundable; that one should carefully monitor the
desire to seek private education for Section A of the grand-
stand, but that I would be happy to have them if they qualified scholastically.

Following that, we toured the school, the curriculum, the chapel policy, and probably City Hall. I thought I
never was going to get back to my tennis game. I was convinced that she had understood me fully. I spoke in native
modern English.

We did the whole drill again the next week. I assured
her I was sympathetic with her financial limitations, but that
the choice was simple. In or out. Tuition was not negotiable.
She chose "In" for the whole tribe, signed the agreements
and wrote the registration check.

Three weeks later, I was blessed with a visit from
Papa. He really didn't want his kids in private school and
would like his money back now, please.

There is something called contractual law, another thing called Board Policy, and a third called survival of the headmistress. Under none of the three was I allowed to give the money back. It was written down. I had shown her, and now I showed him. I suggested he might want to contact the Board. He smiled and left.

In a 1940's movie, calendar pages would waft across the screen to show the passage of time. Time did pass. I was presiding over a faculty meeting in late September when I noticed a frantic semaphore message from my faithful secretary, Tonto, denoting that it was mandatory to interrupt the faculty meeting. That is tantamount to stopping the rotation of the earth. I did. Stepping outside the door I gazed right into the abject eyes of a deputy sheriff, complete with pig iron on his hip. Sooner would he eat grass than do this, Ma'am, but he had to do his duty. Gulping noticeably, he produced from his pocket a warrant for my arrest.

On a clear day you could have heard me in Texas City. Poor fellow had never arrested a headmistress before and he had this feeling that, if not God, at least the Archbishop of Canterbury was going to appear and smite him for his indiscretion. Neither of the above was available so I filled in for them. My citation read that I failed to refund the gentleman's registration fees.

There are a lot of disadvantages to being headmistress — take for example getting arrested at faculty meeting — but lack of access to law firms is not one of them. By the time I was through squalling, everybody short of the attorney general had been alerted. We filed cross action for the remaining tuition. I thought it was a right classy ploy showing utter fearlessness.

The attorneys did their part and I did mine. Everybody knows you have to appear in court in a navy blue Adele Simpson with a white piqué collar. I got mine. Next, I had to decide about the family. Should I inform them of my impending ordeal or tough it out alone? Surely, I thought, it is

60

not fitting that an Erskine should go to the slammer unshriven and unmourned. I called.

The courtroom looked a little like a Colonial Dames meeting. Mama had gathered the aunts, known affectionately in South Texas as the Pixilated Sisters. They were a little hazy on exactly why they were mustering, but they would have gone to a buzzard shoot if family were involved. They were joined by assorted friends who heard they were in town. Thomas Jefferson probably presented Aaron Burr with such a gathering when he picked up his army and moved west.

My legal department was formidable. Everybody wandering through the halls of the courthouse that day dropped in. Half the legals in town are on the Board and the other half have been. I mentioned to each that I would feel comforted by his presence. The plaintiff represented himself. It was sort of like Clarence Darrow vs. W. C. Fields.

I had the good sense to say "yes" twice and "no" once and hush. Solomon-like in his wisdom, the judge ruled that Trinity need not refund the registration. I was remanded to the custody of the immediate world. It was a victory of sorts. The ladies in the front row clapped their white gloves together and we all went home.

I would like to say that we all lived happily ever after. It is not strictly true. Every summer it is a new kook with a new dodge. That is the reason I say to you in all earnestness, STAY AWAY FROM YOUR OFFICE IN JULY. July is the month of kooks.

5

S OME DAYS IT JUST DOESN'T WORK. I KNEW I WAS IN BAD TROUBLE WHEN THE BROWN FILM TYPE-WRITER RIBBON GOT A BACKLASH SOMEWHERE AROUND THE CORONAMATIC 2500 BUTTON, AND IT TOOK ME ALL AFTERNOON TO UNTANGLE IT. MY FEARS WERE COMPOUNDED WHEN I FOUND MYSELF ADJUDI-CATING SUCH MATTERS OF IMPORT AS THE CHEETOS PAPERS BEING ALL OVER THE PLAYGROUND. THE FACT WAS, I SIMPLY DIDN'T HAVE ANYTHING TO SAY THIS MONTH. THAT'S A TERRIBLE TRUTH TO BE FACED BY SOMEONE FORMERLY BILLED AS THE MOUTH OF THE GUADALUPE. ANOTHER CASE OF THE DRY-MOUTH.

I slogged home to turn on the afternoon news and lapse into lethargy. Instead I lapsed into a frothing rage. I watched the first Congressman since the Recent-Unpleas-antness-of-1865 be expelled from the House of Representa-tives. I watched it in its entirety and, during the Congress-man's lengthy statement, I noticed two outstanding things.

The first was that his plea for due process appeared to be based not on his denial of the charges but on his pro-testations that when he took the money he really didn't in-tend to provide the services he promised. Ergo, he was not guilty. Pop Quiz: Would you say that his education had been in (a) a value-centered curriculum, or (b) the popular hu-man secularism rampant in school systems today?

The second thing I noticed was that in making his plea before this august body, he made sixteen glaring gram-matical errors. I do not mean that he incorrectly used the pluperfect subjunctive. Not since Nell Sparks' reign at Seguin

High School have I found anyone who could wrestle that to the ground. I mean he couldn't get a plural subject with a plural predicate in a simple declarative sentence.

I think this hit me hardest because my own school, which makes a fetish of subjects and predicates (my own prose notwithstanding), is suffering the slings and arrows of outrageous fortune this year. We raised the tuition substantially. It eliminated some we did not wish to eliminate. It did not cover little contingencies like the astronomical rise in utilities or the fact that just getting the lights working in acceptable fashion this year cost $1,000. And there was nothing basically wrong with the lights. Planned parenthood and the economy have taken their toll.

To add to my discomfort, the *Wall Street Journal* came out today with a front-page article giving the price of raising a child. To keep a child under your roof until he is eighteen and then send him to a public university will run about $85,000. Nowhere in the breakdown was there an allocation for private Episcopal schools on islands in the Gulf of Mexico. My spirits were dragging.

In Camelot they whistled, sang and danced to keep their spirits up. I prefer to resort to *Cliff Notes* when I am in a course over my head. Even for my dilemma there was direction. A book I found recently, by Paul Dickson, entitled *The Official Rules*, promised a definitive, annotated collection of laws, principles and instructions for dealing with the real world. Eagerly I perused it.

Indeed, there was help. To understand the Congressman's point of view I find Cohen's Law: "What really matters is the name you succeed in imposing on the facts — not the facts themselves."

Or perhaps Bartz' Law of Hokey Horsepuckery: "The more ridiculous the belief system, the higher the probability of its success."

If all else fails, I suggest to him Comin's Law: "People will accept your idea much more readily if you tell them

Benjamin Franklin said it first."

For the comfort of disgruntled headmistresses, I submit the law propounded by Derek Bok of Harvard University: "If you think education is expensive — try ignorance."

Then it was incumbent upon me to find a guideline to help implement my view. It went against my nature to reject it, but I eschewed the motto of Canada Bill Jones: "A Smith and Wesson beats four aces," and chose instead the advice of General Creighton Abrams: "When eating an elephant, take one bite at a time."

6

I'M WAITING FOR THE OTHER SHOE TO DROP. IT'S THE WEEK BEFORE CHRISTMAS AND ALTHOUGH I CAN'T SAY THINGS ARE EXACTLY CALM, I'M HAVING A WONDERFUL TIME IN THE TURMOIL. THAT'S JUST PLAIN ABNORMAL.

The stockings are not yet hung by the chimney with care, but the turkey dressing is made. With old age your priorities change.

The Christmas pageant is in rehearsal and Mary does not have a black eye, Joseph has not opted out in a fit of pique because he wants to be a cow, and Gabriel has not missed rehearsal in favor of a soccer game. Each of these traumas I have faced at one time or another, but not this year. I haven't heard anyone call the second king's present Frankenguntz all season. It's a weird year.

Dickens weekend has just passed. It is rivaled for frivolity only by Mardi Gras. This year we threw in a couple of extra parties for brides. I expected to awaken Monday in the sure and certain knowledge that I was suffering from terminal collapse. Instead, I broke dawn with a stick and finished the week in a dead run.

Cynthia Mitchell is having Trinity School to tea at the Tremont House tomorrow. The Houston Ballet will be there in *Nutcracker* costume to entertain. I knew the children would love it. Dressing ours up in coats and ties or white gloves and patent leather Mary Janes goes big with grandmothers, but I'm astounded at the number of daddies that have signed on. So is the Tremont House. They are laying in a supply of fishes and loaves. We were expecting a hundred maybe and got 400.

It's my turn to do Christmas dinner, speaking of the fishes and the loaves. The family now fills Section A of the stadium. I may not even have a dishwasher. I ought to be panicked. Instead, I'm delighted. Maybe it's delirium. Anyway, it's worth it to be able to say to Christian and Michael, our two newborns this year, "Welcome to Christmas dinner at the home of your great-great-great-grandfather."

The storybooks say this is the way things are supposed to be this time of year, but the Ghost of Christmas Past reminds me daily to look out for the other shoe. It is an unheard of state of grace to be finished, calm and happy on December 15.

"What could possibly go awry?" you ask. Well, for one thing, I have to waltz with the Mouse King tomorrow. I am muttering to myself, "Don't lead. Don't lead."

I recently visited my old college roommate, Jo. We've been through lots together through the years After discussing our present situations, I remarked to her that we'd better remember that day. She was well and happy and so were her family. I was well and happy and so were mine. Furthermore, neither of us was broke. That was, of course, before the Christmas bills began arriving. With any luck at all that shoe that's waiting to drop got lost in the closet in the memorable Fall of '85. I fervently hope so.

7

DIARY OF A HEADMISTRESS: WHOEVER SAID, "THESE ARE THE TIMES THAT TRY MEN'S SOULS," HAD TO HAVE BEEN IN THE SCHOOL RACKET. FURTHERMORE, IT MUST HAVE BEEN THE LAST WEEK OF SCHOOL. I RELAY TO YOU THE EVENTS OF MY LAST TEN DAYS WITHOUT EVEN BOTHERING TO CHANGE NAMES TO PROTECT THE INNOCENT. THERE AREN'T ANY INNO-CENT. IF IT READS A LOT LIKE THE STATIONS OF THE CROSS, I BEG YOUR INDULGENCE.

MONDAY: The calendar for closing school is so crowded we have to Scotch tape a couple of legal pad pages to it to get everything written down. My faithful secretary, Tonto, catches a flaming case of the Infectious Ugh and takes off for a week's R & R in Colorado.

TUESDAY: My talented sixth-grade teacher accepts a job as headmistress of a school in another city. I am delighted for her, but somewhat dismayed at the prospect of replacing her. Nobody is totally irreplaceable, but she ranks among the ten most likely.

WEDNESDAY: End of school bedlam begins with the Pre-school Musicale, followed in rout order by an epidemic of the Sixth-Grade Smarts which is cured only by the suspension of one ringleader and one pilot fish.

THURSDAY: The old chocolate candy/Ex-Lax caper reappears in the second grade. There are no fatalities. Five-thirty P.M.: Kick-off cocktail party for the fund drive workers at Headmistress's house. It is a late evening.

FRIDAY: I check the obituary column and find that I am not listed. Reluctantly, I proceed to school for what I fervently hope will be a slow day. It goes at a pace usually reserved for fire trucks and ambulances. I stomp out grass fires all day long and find three o'clock mercifully approaching as I lean against the door jamb in the hall.

Yul Brenner made a fortune singing something about times when you doubt those things you absolutely know. I stare in awestruck wonder as I see a figure in cutoffs so abbreviated they defy the laws of physics, a tank top, and knee-high roller skates ascend my carpeted stair and trip daintily down the upstairs hall. I am nearsighted enough to have a driver's license restriction. Surely this accounts for it, but, nonetheless, in hot pursuit I overtake the errant skater as she reaches the fourth-grade room.

I hear myself hysterically screeching, "*It's a parent! Whoever thought I would be chasing a parent in roller skates down the upstairs hall?*" She turns, and smiling sweetly says, "I just came to pass out the party invitations."

That's another no-no. Utterly defeated, I nod docilely and retreat down the stairs. Having completed her appointed rounds in record time, she trips down the same stair and serenely skates between the assembled Mothers' Mafia and out the door without further word. A stunned silence ensues.

Nor does the weekend offer surcease. You see, it's about this kid I helped raise who is (a) going to be married shortly, and (b) going to teach for me next year. The wedding festivities are so extensive I find myself having to eat between bites to cover all the parties, but Aunt Budgie gallantly suits up.

MONDAY: Honors Day, Green-Gold Games, and picnic on the Garth. This year we have Medieval Day as a theme. I didn't suspect that King Arthur had a shaving cream toss at his court, or that the sixth grade would draw swords and swash and buckle through the hibiscus bushes. It is the last annual Medieval Day at Trinity School.

TUESDAY: Commencement Day. We practice all morning between frantic forays to check on the progress of the altar piece being constructed from all our cherished school possessions, such as books, basketballs and hockey sticks, and trophies we have won this year. It is terribly impressive, but the Empire State Building was raised with fewer structural problems. We also run out of covers for the Commencement programs. At this point it is a minor crisis.

Commencement is truly gorgeous with two hundred children doing a magnificent job of "Evensong." The Bishop smiles. The parents glow. I beam, hug kids, and break for the exit at the first politely possible moment to head for home and open the door to the throng who have come to celebrate the end of school and visit with the Bishop. He happens to have been our former rector. It is a cast of thousands. I saw 125 glasses put into service in short order. At 1:30 A.M., when the last hard core of revelers suggest that perhaps it is time to go home, I agree with embarrassing haste.

WEDNESDAY: Surely with no kids in the tent and the glow of good fellowship still wafting through the trees there can be no problems, she vainly prays. The patron saint of headmistresses is involved in a crap game somewhere and replies to my prayers with an absent-minded, "Trinity Who?" At this unseen signal, the Spanish teacher approaches in tears, inconsolable because the other Spanish teacher is teaching in Cuban Spanish while she is speaking pure Mexico City Spanish. I point out that the kids are not likely to become United Nations translators upon graduation from Trinity. They will be lucky to say knife, fork, spoon, and thank you, and that I really don't give a rap in what accent they say it.

The music teacher decides to request an exclusion on her contract. She requests to be excused from playing at public worship services or teaching kids the canticles. I handle that with steely-eyed stiletto-tongued brevity. I know some Medal of Honor winners that aren't brave enough to suggest that exclusion to an Episcopal school.

And the freight company delivers fifty-eight cartons of books for next year.

I, Elizabeth Erskine Hollamon, Headmistress, take a paralyzed oath that all of the above is a true and faithful representation of the events of the last ten days at Trinity School, Galveston. Said Headmistress further testifies that the next gentle soul that simpers sweetly that they know how much she is going to miss the challenging and invigorating days of the school year is going to get five in the bicuspids.

8

I AM SUFFERING FROM A SEVERE ATTACK OF *STAN-DARDS* THIS WEEK. I CAUGHT THIS MALADY BECAUSE THERE'S A LOT OF IT GOING AROUND. I SPENT MONDAY IN AUSTIN AT A BOARD MEETING OF THE LICENSING DIVISION OF THE DEPARTMENT OF HUMAN RESOURCES. I ACCEPTED THIS POSITION A FEW YEARS AGO WHEN THEY WERE CONSIDERING LICENSING SCHOOLS. THE FOX WAS INVITED TO WATCH THE HEN HOUSE. I REMAIN THERE BECAUSE THE NEW GENERATION OF APPOINTEES HAVEN'T FIGURED OUT YET THAT THERE IS A PHARISEE AMONG THEM.

The set of standards up for review concerned registered homes. That is the nomenclature for an operation catering to more than our own kid and less than a multitude. The committee proceeded on the premise that since these exist they must be regulated because obviously nobody has sense enough to run their own operation to the satisfaction of their customers and themselves without the divine guidance of a bureaucracy.

One proposal standard ran thusly: *No more than six children may be kept at one time excluding the provider's own children and any school age siblings of the children being kept.* Do you have any idea how many people to expect? Does it matter provided they are well taken care of?

For drop-in centers we pondered the following: *If a child arrives at the center between 6:00 A.M. and 6:00 P.M. the center staff must not allow the child to stay in the center longer than 4 1/2 hours. . .* If you're planning to play a couple of sets of tennis and eat lunch with the girls some

71

Thursday you're out of luck. It might take longer than 4 ½ hours and then Little Oswald would have to meet you on the street corner 'cause he'd been evicted from the drop-in center. I expect the next standard to read, "Only fourteen (14) angels may sit on the head of a pin."

I am sure it is generally necessary to salvation to have some set of standards, but must we legislate to obfuscation? It is possible to write a pretty good set of standards rather clearly. I found an example in the 20th Chapter of a little road book called *Exodus*. They ran this way:

> *You shall have no other gods before me.*
> *You shall not make for yourself any idol.*
> *You shall not take the name of the Lord your God in vain.*
> *Remember to keep holy the Sabbath day.*
> *Honor your father and mother.*
> *You shall not kill.*
> *You shall not commit adultery.*
> *You shall not steal.*
> *You shall not bear false witness against your neighbor..*
> *You shall not covet.*

Now those, Rocky, are standards. Clear. Concise. Unequivocal. Sixty-seven words total. I do not find a list of variances for waiver. It does not say, "You shall not commit adultery except in months containing R's, during the vernal equinox, and when the wind is blowing from the left."

I am also engaged in responding to an accreditation questionnaire aimed at documenting that the standards of the organization have been dutifully upheld throughout the intervening decade. It is comprehensive, to say the least. The 1972 edition weighed twelve pounds upon completion and this promises to shatter the record. It will, that is, if I can ever get it finished. I am having some trouble deciphering the questions. One to which I must reply reads, *How do you identify your minorities?*

I suppose it is bad form to answer, "You look at them, you ninny. The ones with sari's and jewels in their foreheads

72

are Indians. They are a minority in Galveston. The black ones are called Negroes. Regardless of quantity they are still considered a minority for reasons best known to the United States government. Hazem Ahmed and Nael Al-Abdullah could probably pass for a minority in South Texas if not in Cairo."

Surely I have missed the point. Surely they want some high and lofty reply. They follow that inquiry with the request to know how we provide for these minorities. We provide for them by teaching them to read and write and count just like we do the rest of the kids. We don't identify minorities. We identify kids.

Further down the list we find, *Provide evidence that your faculty knows the rules and regulations of the School.* I don't know how to do that. I can show the Grand Inquisitors where it is written down and sign affidavits as to when it was all discussed, but unless there is a flagrant shattering of the rules followed by abject protestations that the offender didn't know, I can't provide evidence. He's innocent until proven guilty. I also cannot provide evidence that they have not coveted their neighbor's house, etc., etc. I'd just rather not know how they stand with some of the rest of the commandments.

There is nothing to be done about standards and committees. They are a fact of life like sand fleas. Sooner or later some committee will take a perfectly clear statement and qualify it out of existence. Not even God went unscathed. Nonsense, you say? Read the 21st Chapter of *Exodus* and then argue.

Lord, grant me the patience to accept those things which I cannot change, the courage to change those things which I can change, and the wisdom to know the difference.

9

IT IS OCTOBER 28, 1981. THROUGHOUT AMERICA CATHODE TUBES ARE HEATING UP SO CLEAR-EYED, RED-BLOODED FOLK CAN WATCH THE SIXTH, AND POSSIBLY DECIDING, GAME OF THE WORLD SERIES. NOT MINE, HOWEVER. MY TV IS HOOKED UP TO A CABLE THAT WORKS ONLY ON FEAST DAYS AND HOLIDAYS. APPARENTLY TODAY IS NEITHER OF THE ABOVE.

It's not that I am an avid devotee of baseball. When players went on strike I hardly noticed, but I do enjoy the Series if only because when rained out we get reruns of "Laverne and Shirley."

Having graphically explained that to Cablevision, kicked the chair and done the laundry, I settled down to while away the time with the reading that I rarely get to do at school. I had five *Wall Street Journals* and a little publication called *Education Week* to wend my way through. I was diligent.

Before I had gotten up to Tuesday I had already developed severe Educator's Syndrome. This malady comes from a surfeit of cotton-candy prose about tuition tax credits and apologia on whatever portion of the school system the writer is concerned with this week. No. 8, Vol. I concerns itself with high schools.

A gentleman named Theodore Sizer, hardly an unknown in education circles, has devoted himself to a study of American high schools entitled, inventively, *A Study of American High Schools*.

Mr. Sizer said he puts little stock in the prevailing theory that high schools have gotten out of control. You

74

have to understand that Mr. Sizer is not the principal of P. S. 13. He is the Headmaster of Phillips Academy at Andover, Massachusetts. That might account for his point of view. Mr. Sizer continued, "In fact, a contrary argument can be made that many of the perceived problems of high schools are the side effects of the school's historic successes." Does that sound like the estate executor explaining why your half of the cotton died this year?

This massive research was financed by the Carnegie Foundation and a couple I wish I had met first named Ester A. and Joseph Klingenstein. They paid the piper to the tune of $882,000.

The next paragraph outlines a study by John I. Goodlad, a name known to every education school undergraduate, which is nearing its conclusion after a decade-long study. It is entitled *A Study in Schooling.* Care to guess what that cost?

So far today, I have spent nine hours hassling with a variety of problems ranging from revising the music curriculum to transporting temporary buildings to Trinity to relieve the overcrowded situation in the Middle School. Any one of them could have been marvelously, inventively solved with $882,000 from Ester A. and Joseph Klingenstein.

I recently received a less than flattering fan letter from a very eloquent lady who traced my genealogy from cynic to misanthrope. I really wish I could reply in sparkling repartee, but I must agree. Tonight all I can say is, "You named it, Ace." But, you see, like falling test scores and uneducated educational products, it really isn't my fault. It is the fault of malfunctioning technological equipment.

I wish I knew how the Dodgers were doing.

10

THE TREATISE TODAY, MY CHILDREN, IS ON THE SUBJECT OF GODMOTHERHOOD. I SPEAK UNCHALLENGED AS AN EXPERT IN THE FIELD. I HAVE FIFTEEN GODCHILDREN — AND I THINK THEY ARE ALL GETTING MARRIED THIS WEEK. PERHAPS IT ONLY SEEMS THIS WAY. WHEN REQUIRED RECENTLY BY THE PRE-SCHOOL MAFIA TO NAME THE DAYS OF THE WEEK, I HEARD MYSELF REPLY, "JANUARY, FEBRUARY, MARCH . . ." IT IS A FUNCTION OF OLD AGE — OR PERHAPS GODMOTHERHOOD.

Do not enter this hallowed state lightly or ill-advisedly. It requires some outlay of time and effort and not inconsiderable shekels, but as we say in the trade, it's a great learning experience.

Just the other day — about twenty years ago — I held one on my lap at the card table. Her grandfather had little faith in my ability to lead her in the paths of Christian righteousness. He even had the temerity to question whether I'd taught her her prayers. I had been working at it daily, so with complete confidence I cued this two-year-old into her act.

"Tell your grandfather what I taught you," I smirked.

Without a moment's hesitation and in a voice clearly audible in Kerrville, she replied, "High, Low, Jack and the Game!"

"No," I screamed. "The other one, the other one."

Her intrepid and immediate response was, "Frosty, Man, Frosty."

Well, you can't win them all. I have continued to ply

her with my godmotherly wisdom. She marries this month. I think she's got it right when they ask, "Do you take this man . . ."

Another one marries Friday. I was on the receiving committee when she came out of the delivery room. I changed her diapers, gave her her first spanking and basked in godmotherly glory when she progressed to Good Shepherd Nursery School. As I arrived one day for my Friday frappé, she crawled in my lap and regaled me with episodes of school life.

"We went to Big Church today," she said.

"Oh," said I happily. "What did you do there?" This was before I got in the headmistress racket and was not one of the cognoscenti about chapel.

"Well," she said, "We put on our chapel caps and then we lined up two-by-two and marched over to Big Church. We knelt down and said a prayer and then Mr. B. told us a story."

Pursuing this interchange to its ecclesiastical conclusion, I continued, "What did he tell you?"

"He said Jesus got lost and Joseph couldn't find him and you kids keep quiet."

There was one time, like the Little Tailor with the Fly Swatter, that I got three in one pop. Jason, Joe, and Joshua. Jason and Josh were twins. Joey was ten months older. Their mother taught for me. It was a private christening, as anyone could understand who knew Joey, Jason, and Josh. The sun shone magnificently through the gorgeous Sealy window depicting Jesus with little children coming unto him. They decided against coming unto him just as I was renouncing the devil and all his works and began scampering in three directions among the pews. The service disintegrated into a rodeo with six of us bulldogging and presenting them screaming at the baptismal font. They live in California now. Joey is quarterback and Jason and Josh play guards. I have it on good authority that they even go to Sunday School.

One weekend I arrived at Love Field to find my good friend tight-jawed.

"What's the matter?" I tentatively inquired.

"Your godson got thrown out of nursery school today," she replied as if I were personally responsible.

"How come?" I inquired, incredulous.

"He wouldn't come in from sand pile."

Children, I tell you in great earnestness, godmothers should not laugh in such times of crisis. It adds fuel to the fire and kids could get creamed. Even little kids. Don't laugh.

But godmotherhood is not all fun and games. You have to have talent too. One must learn how to sit through endless Little League ball games without going mad and biting yourself. You have to suit up for that ritual wringing of the hands known as Rush Week, and it helps to know how to sew sequins for those regional rhinestone festivals like Cotton Palace and Fiesta. Mainly, you have to be available. One of mine is spending the spring in Spain. It's hard to be available there. I suggest a lot of stock in AT&T.

I like weddings about as much as the next fella. I am in the championship flight when it comes to drinking toasts, but I'd rather drink them at somebody else's godchild's wedding. I'm not through playing with the toys yet. Some Eastern sage probably said it. It may be an Indian Veda. Godchildren soon grow up. Godmothers rarely do.

78

11

EVERYBODY AGREES. IT'S PRACTICALLY A TENET OF THE FAITH. WITHIN THEIR OWN DOMAIN THERE IS NO MORE POWERFUL ENTITY THAN A HEADMISTRESS. FOR EXHIBIT A, LET ME PRESENT MISS HOCKADAY. When I attended her school I would have bet that she could have exerted imperial will while washing up in the cafeteria. I tried to follow suit. I wear my blue blazer with the Trinity patch even when I go out to lunch. I ignore those smart alecks that claim I have been out to lunch for years. It is beneath me to reply. What care I that I look like the half-size section of the Talbot catalog. It shows dedication. It is trooping the color. Where then, I ask you, did I go wrong? What happened to my imperial image? *Why* won't they let me pick the music for the Christmas pageant?

It is true that my ear is slightly metallic and I possess less than perfect pitch. This came to my attention a few years ago when one of my classes invited me to carol. The invitation was classic. It was delivered this way. "Pick a note you like a lot and practice up so you can come pretty close every time and we'll let you go caroling with us." I sent cookies and declined.

My music department is highly professional and very talented. They know my devotion to Walt Kelly's state of the art parody on Christmas carols and harbor a fear that I will whip out the Pogo Christmas Book and swing into "Deck the Halls with Boston Charlie" or "Good King Wenceslaus Looked Out on His Feets Uneven." I was going to do nothing of the kind. All I wanted was to include "Hark the Herald Angels Sing." I don't think that is asking too much.

"Hark the Herald Angels Sing" must be written in a funny key because it is the only carol where I can stay on tune through the whole verse. I deny categorically that it is a dumb carol. In fact, it's a rung or two above some. I have been singing "God Rest Ye Merry Gentlemen" for more decades than I care to count and I don't know what that means yet.

We call our school program at Trinity a traditional lesson and carol service. The lessons are traditional, but I don't know about the carols. In Guadalupe County we didn't sing "Il Le Nee" a lot. And down at St. Andrew's we didn't even know that "Saw You Never in the Twilight" was a carol. I don't think Miss Mary Gilmore could play that. And never anywhere in recorded history could we find a sixth-grade boy and girl to do the duet, "Joseph Dearest, Joseph Mine." But we were very good on "Hark the Herald Angels Sing."

So I flunked Imperial Will. I won't let it ruin my Christmas. I will give in gracefully and learn all the words to "I See a Rose Tree Springing" and the new tune to the "Magnificat." My three hundred twenty angels will perform magnificently before an admiring audience of parents. I will smile on them and hug them and bid them Merry Christmas. Then I shall throw presents in the car and race toward I-10 so I can get to St. Andrew's for midnight service. At midnight service at St. Andrew's we always sing "Hark the Herald Angels Sing." Merry Christmas.

12

S O MUCH FOR THE PUBLISHING BUSINESS. I RETIRE FROM IT IN ITS ENTIRETY. MY FORAYS INTO THE FIELD HAVE BEEN SPORADIC AT BEST. TWO OR THREE TIMES A YEAR I GUSSY UP, FIRE UP OLE BLUE, AND TAP OUT A TRINITY NEWSLETTER. A GOOD MANY OF YOU RECEIVE THEM.

I will concede that they are a tad Down Home, but they are newsy, and they do pay off like a slot machine. Rarely have I published a wish list that the goods didn't promptly ring in like freedom, so it is motivated as much by avarice as it is the need to communicate. Well, kiss it all goodby. I'm just not up to it.

At Christmastime one has to have a newsletter. The President of the Board has to wish everybody happy holiday, the new teachers and new Board have to be introduced, and all the magnificent accomplishments of the students have to be outlined so that when fathers and grandfathers make their year-end financial decisions we will be fresh on their minds. Thus sayeth the moneychanger down at the temple.

We take checks on December 31, 32 and 33. That's legal, isn't it? But it means that newsletters have to go out before December 33rd, so I sat down and wrote one. It was perhaps my finest hour even if you toss in the last year's Christmas article that *Episcopalian* just bought.

I contracted with the printer for a delivery date. I am naive, but I'm not just pig-ignorant stupid. I have negotiated with printers before. This one is a nice man but, you see, he is a printer, and their veracity is usually questionable.

I am convinced that all printers had the measles in second grade when schools were teaching how to tell time. It may be a requirement for their union card.

Have you ever assembled mothers to do a mailing on the week before Christmas and not had the newsletter show up? I rank it in popularity somewhere between shock treatment and a root canal. No ninny I, I put the mailing date two days after promised delivery. Still not smothered in confidence, I called daily from Friday to Monday to be reassured that I would, indeed, get the newsletter on schedule.

Come Monday at 9:00 A.M. the phone rang. Could I postpone the mailing committee an hour? We postponed it all day. Tuesday at 9:00 A.M., same story. I assured him in dulcet tones that if that newsletter was not at my desk at 9:00 A.M. on Wednesday, I would cross the causeway with meat cleaver in hand and it would truly be him and me. He understands native modern English.

Wednesday dawns, pageant practice begins, mothers assemble, phone rings. Newsletter late, but coming, oh so shortly. I offer to come get it. He frantically says he'll send it. I wonder at the tone of voice, but not for long. What, I ask myself, would a well-meaning printer with a healthy sense of self-preservation do in a case like that? He would lie. Six, two, and even. The newsletter ain't even hit the presses yet.

Smiling at the Mother's Mafia in hallway assembled, pouring coffee, offering candy and doing the Old Soft Shoe, I disappear at intervals to call for a progress report. At 10:30 I am assured that the newsletters are on the way. At 11:30 I report that they are not here. At 12:30 I announce my intention of finding that wayward student who has left two hours before in a brown van filled with newsletters, for obviously there is trouble afoot.

At 1:15 I arrive at the printing shop, a millimeter from apoplexy. Well, he said, the student was afraid she was going to have car trouble and had returned. I pointed out that she could have played a round of golf and walked home in the intervening time. Where were the newsletters? They were, he said, residing in a taxicab on their way to Galveston. All that time the Mothers' Mafia has remained assembled in the hall, muttering invectives and wishing they were Christmas shopping.

At 2:15 newsletters have still not arrived. I give up on the printer and call the cab company. That ethnic automotive society has routed the driver by Hitchcock to drop a fare, thence through Alta Loma, probably to play a set of tennis, and at the moment the dispatcher has no idea when the courier will arrive in Galveston. I apologize to the mothers and send them off to their appointed rounds.

At 2:30, fifty-three hours after their promised time, newsletters arrive. I grab one to see how they came out. It is painfully evident that they came out garbled. It is printed so that the faculty picture is rent in twain by the insert page which results in the information that our new music teacher is married to the Space Dance Theater which was furnished to Trinity School courtesy of the Cultural Arts Council.

Have you ever wondered why the Magi mounted their camels and headed out across the desert in the middle of a winter night? They had just seen the proofs of their latest newsletter and left in pursuit of the errant printer. Along the way they encountered the newborn Christ Child and paused to worship Him. Saving the life of an itinerant Arab printer was Jesus's first and least-known miracle. It was the only mistake in an otherwise perfect life.

13

THAT'S THE WAY IT IS WITH THE MONTH OF AU-GUST. ONE CAN MISS "HICKORY STICK" DEAD-LINES AND NEVER EVEN SNAP TO IT. I WAS BUILD-ING BUILDINGS. DON'T ASK ME WHAT I KNOW ABOUT BUILDING. I CAN ONLY TELL YOU THAT IT IS A LOT MORE THAN I KNEW IN JUNE. WE DID GET OUR NEW ANNEX DEDI-CATED ON AUGUST 29 AMID CHEERS AND REJOICING.

There were a few things left undone that we ought to have done. The hot water was cold, the panic bars did not respond to panic and the electric timer caused the building to be lit like the Kennedy Center at night and dark as purgatory during the day. Always choose a board president with building experience and those things will get worked out.

September is a walk in the park. It's either done or not by then and prayer and fasting will not help. Just go on planning high and lofty events such as Episcopal School Week, fund raisings and, oh yes — Blessing of the Pets.

I think Sally Woolrich is responsible for my knowing about the blessing of the pets. She's at St. Francis and she would know about things like that. I could have remained blessedly ignorant forever but I always look at what Sally is doing. At St. Francis they bless pets on St. Francis Day. Imitation is the sincerest form of flattery. I blessed pets.

The first time I did this the horse broke from his moorings, the big Airedale chose to pursue the twitching little bunny across the play yard and the muskrat was lost forever among the garbage cans in the outer environs. Right off you can see how I love it. Some years when I have been noble, brave and true I am rewarded by having St. Francis

Day come on the weekend. Nineteen-eighty-two is not one of my vintage years. Staunchly I remember my childhood and prepare to bless pets.

Some things are the undisputable and inalienable right of headmistresses, and declaring the ground rules is one of them. I declare snakes unblessable. Don't argue or use logic on me. I am scared witless of snakes and won't have them on any playground. Period. Eels are out, too.

The Blessing of the Pets does not have the universal appeal of, say, Christmas or Parents Night. I quote for you a letter I received some years ago about the annual festival.

Dear Budgie,

I cannot help but notice the great publicity which the Blessing of Animals has received. I demand equal time. I base this request on the following story:

Some infidel threw over our back fence a small, ugly, starved, adolescent kitten. When my daughter was told that she could not keep the animal, she took it next door and gave it to a neighbor. Each day thereafter, she went over to pet it. Now this kitten may be ugly but it is not dumb and very soon found its way to our house daily. After long discussion and fervent promises that she would always take care of the cat, Elizabeth was permitted to keep this animal. With time and nourishment it grew in intelligence and stature, but not in wisdom. I'm sad to say one day it crawled into the motor compartment of my wife's station wagon. When she turned on the engine, the cat got caught in the fan. When I came home, she informed me that she thought that the cat had gotten caught in the fan, but that she could not be sure because she could not find the cat and she did not have the courage to open up the hood. Therefore, I went out and found a great deal of fur scattered all over the underside of the hood of the car. Subsequently, the cat was found in a state of injury which prompted me, as a wise physician, to tell my children that the cat should be left alone, that it would die that night.

Four days later, I discovered my children were feeding this animal secretly, that it had developed gangrene on its completely skinned tail and still had a broken appendage. Therefore, on Labor Day, we made a special trip to the vet. (I should tell you that a Labor Day emergency call to the veterinarian's office is an expensive endeavor.) I gave the high sign to the veterinarian that the cat would probably die and wasn't that sad, but that he should see if he could save it. I cannot imagine how he could have misinterpreted my signals that the cat was to be put to sleep. He did so, however, and three weeks later, following rectal drains, casts on legs, amputation of tail, multiple x-rays, and gallons of antibiotics, this vision of loveliness was retrieved from the veterinarian and taken home. I should tell you that prior to being able to retrieve this cat, I had to pay the veterinarian in excess of $330. To further the insult, I have discovered since that the injury to this cat was not all in the region of the tail. Its movement with that fan must have involved the other end also. Now . . . I think that you can understand that I deserve equal time and could probably find other similarly inclined parents who would join me.

14

THE ROAD TO HUMILITY IS NOT WELL TRAVELED. I BYPASS IT AS OFTEN AS I CAN. SOMETIMES, HOWEVER, THINGS SIMPLY CROWD UP ON ME. THIS WEEK THEY OUGHT TO BE PENALIZED FIFTEEN YARDS FOR PILING ON.

The last couple of weeks I've had more guests than Conrad Hilton with about as much notice. I can usually bob and weave and fake it, but this week I've been caught flat-footed twice and it's only Wednesday.

I returned from Spring Break to find my godchild and her child in residence down the block. I was delighted to see them and especially pleased when my five-year-old grand-godchild decided to come to breakfast before catching the early plane back to Dallas. She arrived unattended at 7:00 A.M. I whipped into gear. "What do you like for breakfast!" I chirped.

She thought she'd choose bacon and eggs from my not too varied menu. Eggs were best basted, we concurred. I don't do that often and, predictably, made rather a mess of it. We discussed alternatives. One logical one was to begin again. Lo, it was not viable. That was the only egg left in the as-yet unreplenished larder. She handled it like a trooper. I dug my toe in the dirt and promised to do better next time. Next time she'll probably bring her own eggs.

That was yesterday. Today at 3:30, I had a call from an old and very dear friend from far away. She was in Houston and could come down for dinner. She would leave soon to avoid the traffic.

I finished up at school as soon as I could and headed home to clear a path. My house is rarely clean, but it's usually picked up. Today it wasn't. The doorbell rang just as I mashed the breakfast dishes in the dish-hider. She'd gotten here post haste because she just took a cab. From Houston. The cab driver waited while we visited and had dinner. Then he returned her to Houston. She hasn't changed in forty years. She's always had more dollars than sense, but I was flattered that she chose time to visit over expense. She could have cared less that the Red Cross was going to begin passing out doughnuts at my house if I didn't reclaim the disaster area soon.

I remind myself that in the great list of priorities there are some things that, on balance, just don't matter. I spent Spring Break on a cruise. Spring Break was also Holy Week. I was amazed and gratified to find that on the ship was John Peabody, retired Dean of the Cathedral in Baltimore. He was holding Episcopal services Palm Sunday and Good Friday. I went. Rocking around in rough seas in the converted theater with an organ that was less than cathedral-like, accompanied by a group of tinny off-key singers, was not your most majestic Holy Week experience, but it was Good Friday service and it was Episcopal. I realized right off that they were my kind of folk when I noticed the message on the front of the pamphlet printed in lovely Old English letters. It said, "Commandment XI. Thou shalt not take this book." Seems he was continuing on shipboard and needed the books for Easter services.

The paucity of pomp bothered me not at all, which is strange for one who loves services with bishops and banners and trumpets and tympani. The fact that the service was there was sheer serendipity. I expect that the scarcity of eggs and the plethora of clutter may fall in the same category. It's having friends here to love and visit with that matters.

So once again, she rationalizes her way from the road to humility. With some of us it's an art form. Only this time I think the rationalization is valid. Well, that's what we sidesteppers always say.

15

I'M THINKING A LOT ABOUT PARENTS THIS MONTH. IT DOESN'T TAKE PINKERTON TO FIND THE REASON. MY MOTHER DIED ON APRIL 10TH. MAMA LIVED A GRACIOUS AND PRODUCTIVE EIGHTY-FOUR YEARS AND EXITED THIS LIFE SERENELY IN THE MIDST OF HER FAMILY. SHE LEAVES A LARGE AND LOVING GROUP WHO CARRY ON HER VALUES AND TRADITIONS AS AN OBLIGATION.

I miss my mother, but I have not lost her. She lives in every decision and in every human relation entered into by her survivors — be they family or that group of near family we lovingly call our Sandpile Buddies. She influenced them all. There are worse legacies to leave.

Was Mama's life and influence unique? I think not. Every parent holds the same sway over his children and his children's friends. On bad days I wonder if parents realize what a responsibility parenthood is. Any adult can develop Sealy Posturepedic Prowess. Procreation bears the same relationship to parenthood that bullfighting bears to agriculture. The first is an athletic aptitude. The second is immortality.

My mother entered this life before the invention of the automobile. Electricity and radio were childhood toys. She casually pointed this out to me in the lobby of the Excelsior Hotel in Florence, as together we watched the moon landing on television. Life certainly changed but have values so substantially changed during the same period?

Apparently not. I work daily with parents of 400 children. Today a greater percentage of them work outside the home. They must be judicious in the expenditure of time for the simple reason that they have less of it. Life in the marketplace presents them with high sounding "issues of magnitude" and "environmental concerns" that are more fascinating than multiplication tables and spelling lists, but they continue to give words and numbers priority because they realize that when one arrives at the second generation of ignorance this country and our values are in big trouble. For that awareness I am eternally grateful.

Trinity, like your school, is striving mightily for the academic excellence that provides a place in the sun for each child. To do this in a church-related — ergo not too affluent — school is a real education gavotte requiring lots of fancy footwork. Only the parents can provide that.

Dr. Don Erikson did a whole, bona fide, scientific study on this and concluded that the difference in survival and non-survival of independent schools depends in very large part on the sense of educational jeopardy felt by parents, and their positive response to it.

I can provide lots of jeopardy, so I find myself today in the middle of a big drive run totally by concerned parents planning to ensure the educational future of their children. I am typing in my office. They are in the parish hall setting up the auction so that Budgie and her babies can get the needed fifty grand.

The parents of Trinity are busy and savvy and wonderful, but they are not unique. The same thing is happening in your school and in schools throughout the country. Parents are taking parenthood very seriously. Sure, there are some who aren't. Television shows them to you daily. People who quietly do their job are not newsworthy. That's an unfortunate deficit in our system. We read about Caesar and Cicero and Livy, but it was the Roman matrons who saved Roman culture. It took a couple of centuries for that to dawn on us.

Today I write in praise of parents: yours, mine, and those of your children and your children's sandpile buddies. These are the people who are quietly, unobtrusively, perpetuating the system of values on which our culture will survive — and it will. There ought to be a Prize for Parenthood. Parents, I salute you.

16

SOME SORRY SONOVAGUN STOLE MY TYPEWRITER. I THINK HE WAS MAKING AN EDITORIAL COMMENT, AND FOR THAT ALONE HE OUGHT TO GO TO JAIL. IT WAS MY FAVORITE TOY. IT TOOK SIX WEEKS TO FIND ONE EXACTLY LIKE IT AND DURING THAT TIME I HAD TO FIND OTHER PROJECTS TO ENTERTAIN ME.

I took my surgeon to dinner as soon as I determined that I would indeed live. Fed him fish. Didn't trust him with anything any sharper than a fish knife.

We had the 32nd annual Leslie Otto Memorial Flower Show. Everybody brings an arrangement. I won second again. You *know* how I feel about second. I'm going to give them one more chance. Next year may be the 33rd and final Flower Show.

The children, showing concern and uncommon good sense, formed a fund in honor of my operation that was to replace the shrubs at the school ruined by Hurricane Alicia and her stepsister, The Freeze. Much flattered, I began a beautification project that made Operation Sparkle look dingy. If cleanliness is next to godliness I might have just ascended. You will notice the particular use of tense.

Yes, Virginia, all did not go as planned. In the great communal owning of the property we arrive at some anomalies. It is the church's roof and the school's carpet. The school got finished first. The new carpet was in place at precisely the time the roofers decided to remove the skylights and spill hot tar on the you-know-what. The pristine new carpet is piebald and the roofers have declared bankruptcy.

As long as I was beautifying, I thought, I might as

well go "todas porkus" and finally at last do something positive about the Busy Bee. You remember the Busy Bee — the eyesore ex-cab station that so valiantly withstood the storm when everything worth while was getting blown down? Surely it would make me feel better to renovate the Busy Bee.

When you've been sick you can get by with a lot. A formerly unsympathetic Board acquiesced. I got a small grant from a friendly foundation and we secured a crew to knock down the unusable part and paint-up-fix-up. They were cheap but trustworthy, the contractor assured me.

They began on Monday. They had this backhoe they had rented for the day and they took turns playing on it. Periodically one or the other would get on it, cowboy around for awhile, and then, with less than expert dexterity, would whale the daylights out of the building with the side of the backhoe. It was effective, if awkward. Awkward is perhaps not the best word. At least it is not the word I used when I watched in fascinated horror as Vladimir took a mighty swing at the Busy Bee — and missed.

If you are going to demolish a building it is better not to own the one next to it. Trinity II received a telling blow that knocked off concrete and sent cracks down the window frames. Vladimir does not have insurance.

There are other ways to do constructive things and I began to feel that perhaps the brick and mortar approach was not mine this month. The mail brought the new "essential elements" from House Bill 246. I thought I would check it out — all 256 pages of it.

Curriculum was much on my mind when I went home and collapsed in front of the TV. "Entertainment Tonight" announced a marvelous education breakthrough — a new way to teach reading to teenagers. My teenagers already know how to read; nonetheless I listened with interest.

The solution to all the problems, Ladies and

Gentlemen, has arrived. We take video cassettes of rock music and put subtitles on them so that the little Einsteins can match the written word to the lyric, and that's the way they will learn to read. I have the feeling that their vocabulary is going to be somewhat limited.

Some days you eat the bear and some days the bear eats you, but regardless of who is chewing, it is very tiring. Tonight I got a call about coming to the Hockaday reunion. I demurred — I hope graciously. They just don't understand about headmistresses this time of year. I wouldn't cross the causeway to take talking movies of the Second Coming.

17

HONORS DAY AT TRINITY IS ONE OF OUR FAVOR-
ITE DAYS. IT IS FUN TO SPEND THE DAY PASSING
OUT AWARDS AND COMPLIMENTS AND THEN
HAVE A PICNIC AND FIELD DAY EVENTS. NOT A DARK
CLOUD ON THE HORIZON TODAY.

Well, perhaps one. I am about as popular as a snake
at a picnic for continuing to have Honors Day on Memorial
Day. Some daddies swear they haven't had a good fishing
trip since their kid started school.

I began Honors Day twelve years ago when it appeared that Commencement was rapidly becoming a three-
day seminar. I made Monday Honors Day, where we did all
the award giving and class singing, and Tuesday Commencement with everybody all shined up and singing "Evensong"
like a bunch of little angels. Now Honors Day has become
the length of a three-day seminar, and I am at a loss to know
where to carve on it. Just dedicate the day and forget it.

I had originally planned to change my format this
year and have our shows on Tuesday and Wednesday. I also
wanted all bishops extant for my first graduating class from
Middle School. I can wield some influence over some things,
but tornados, hurricanes and bishops are out of my realm.
Bishops could only come on Tuesday. Hence, we have commencement on Tuesday. I have only slightly more graduating students than bishops. Then it will be June.

For more years than I care to count the advent of
June meant two things. One was that school ceased and
desisted. The other was that I rounded up the children of
my friends and the friends of my "children" and took them

all to Europe for some designated number of weeks between three and nine, depending on the amount of time I could be gone from school and the state of my finances. I loved it. It gave me a chance to enjoy motherhood, which I did to the fullest until the kids needed new shoes. Then I loved them around the neck and sent them home to papa.

I had all the qualifications of Tour Directorship — an ounce of patience, a soupçon of historical background, and an infinite capacity for orange marmalade. Survivors of European breakfasts know that is the most important one.

This year I am packing my bags shortly after Commencement and dusting off my passport again, but there is one outstanding difference. I'm not the tour director. I confess that it gives me pause. My school has decided that what I really need is about three weeks study at Oxford with a group of English headmasters. This boondoggle was born at a meeting of headmasters of independent schools in Santa Fe last year. It is amazing how many of us have been able to talk our boards into it.

There is a week of free time at the end. That's where the fun is going to begin. A friend, and honorary Board member, is going with me. We have talked to each other three times today. The tour director quadrille has begun. The tour director quadrille is the dance you do when you find yourself with a whole batch of chiefs and no Indians at all trying to decide where to go next. I may have to major in "followership" during this summer semester and I guarantee you that will be the greatest learning experience of my career.

95

18

I AM RE-INVENTING THE WHEEL. EVERY AUGUST I RE-PLACE A SPOKE OR TWO, BUT THIS TIME IT'S "TODAS PORKUS." THE REASONS FOR THIS GREAT REORGA-NIZATION ARE SEVERAL. FIRST, I LOST A LOT OF TEACH-ERS LAST YEAR. SOME HAD BABIES. SOME HAD HUS-BANDS WHOSE JOBS REQUIRED A MOVE. THERE WAS THE UBIQUITOUS GRADUATION FROM MEDICAL SCHOOL, AND A NEW AND INTERESTING ENTRY IN THE FIELD, THE RETURN OF THE FULL-TIME MOTHER.

About thirty percent of my faculty is new. The remaining seventy percent got swapped around to insure stability at every grade level. The result is that *nobody* knows what in blazes is going on.

The second reason for the great renovation is that Trinity is hosting the SAES Conference in October and pride forces me to have this school in the best shape it has been in since it was built. I've polished the silver three times and the party is still months away. I did so much business with the painter this summer that he gave me a birthday present. That ought to tell you something.

When I left for Scotland I had it all neatly put together with the ends tucked in. The faculty was complete, the books were ordered, the painting was done, the carpet laid and the stockings hung by the chimney with care. I was gone two weeks. *Two flippin weeks!* When I returned, the church's carpenter had discovered dry rot in all the window casings on the cloister to the tune of about $7,000, the cleaning service quit, and the coach decided to become a tennis pro. Two flippin weeks. I have danced a tarantella ever since trying to stamp out the grass fires. Things are coming along nicely as of today, but I don't make book on anything.

I called a couple of schools yesterday on SAES business and got the same answer at both. "I'm sorry, Father _____ is on vacation this week." How do they do that? Don't their windows rot in July and their coaches ever decide to join the tour? I think I need to take lessons from them.

And speaking of lessons, when one has a new faculty one must be prepared to spend lots of time giving lessons on How We Do It Here. I don't mind being in the classroom because I feel very much at home there. I feel so at home that I usually take the chalk away and do it myself. I keep muttering to myself that this year I'm really going to watch the teacher. The *other* teacher. I'm a teacher, too.

The orientation part frankly scares me witless. I know how a mother must feel sending her kid off to college for the first time. I have to worry about what I failed to tell them.

Did I do the bit about children being like pot plants? The more you cultivate them and love on them the better they grow.

Did I do my song and dance about speaking to children like you speak to your friends? Did I mention the inadvisability of getting into a shouting match with parents, no matter how wrong they are?

Have I spoken on the expectation of excellence — mine for them, theirs for the student and the student's for himself? Probably I have. I talk about it a lot.

Have I said enough about discipline? How can I explain the difference between a well-run classroom and a student body in little black jackboots goose-stepping down the hall?

I must remember to speak in native modern English. Not everyone speaks Seguinese. It's a pity. Maybe I'll put in a course called "Seguinese as a Second Language." Perhaps I ought to require it for graduation. I had the last faculty speaking it like natives.

Orientation time is tomorrow. I can: (a) stay up all night and worry about it, or (b) bite my nails and wait for the other shoe to fall. My third alternative is (c) to declare that I have done all I can and pack it up and join the Swimming Women at the Parkey's pool. I have every confidence that if there are further words of wisdom to be spoken it will definitely be there. Ergo, I chose (c). Good luck on your opening.

19

I'M ON A HEALTH KICK. I THINK IT'S GOING TO KILL ME. IT'S ALL THE FAULT OF THE SYSTEM. IT'S STRUC-TURED SO THAT IN SEPTEMBER THERE JUST ISN'T MUCH TO DO. THAT'S HOW YOU GET IN TROUBLE.

I explained a year or so ago that September was a serene month for Heads because the work was done and the dike hadn't had time to break yet. Usually I run away to meetings. Sometimes I even learn something. This year, however, I didn't run away because frankly I couldn't afford it. There were those other things that took priority.

We completed restoring the school this summer and even beautified the Busy Bee. It was the house's turn. Lord knows the house needed help. Hoisting a grog to bad weather and storm money, we began work. The storm money does the walls and floors, but the furniture recovering is the responsibility of Ole Moms. There went Wilmington, Delaware, and fund-raiding seminar.

Then there is the church's fund drive for the air-conditioning and such. Ned-In-The-First-Reader knows one must make a pledge one can't afford just to set the right example. There went San Francisco and NAES.

With improvement rampant it seemed only natural to begin a little self-help program. There was certainly plenty of room for that but, perhaps, it was imprudent to cease and desist on drinking and eating at the same time one fires up on exercise. If ever you are tempted to follow this example, I urge you not to announce your intentions to a waiting world because they are all going to help you keep your resolve — even after you've changed your mind about the wisdom of the entire project.

I began with a vengeance. I locked the liquor cabinet and barricaded the wine cellar. I froze everything edible in my entire household, salvaging only string bean strings and tea bags. Neither contain calories. I proceeded to promenade the malls until I procured jogging shoes. It's not my fault that they are pink and grey. Those were the only ones on sale. My visiting brother took one look at them and asked in incredulous tones, "You're not going to wear those outside the house, are you?"

I confess, I don't really jog. That would cause about a nine-point reading on the Richter Scale. I do jiggle a lot.

Seems all the friends who are helping me behave are at least six feet tall. They have a six-inch head start with every stride. They accompany me on my daily exercise rounds just to keep me honest. They saunter along the Seawall and chat while I huff and puff and pedal hard just to stay in shouting distance. I know every trick on the two-mile course. Cutting behind the garbage cans on 53rd St. and Avenue U, I can catch up a step and a half. A step saved is a step earned. I finish second most of the time. Most of the time there are only two of us.

One gets in trouble of this sort in serene September when there isn't much else to do, but this October. . . . Today we had 100 preschoolers go to the zoo. Success comes in many forms. We got home with the same 100 we left with — I think. The fire department pulled up in two huge trucks for their annual fire drill while all the Middle School was at lunch. It looked like the evacuation of Dunkirk. The new roof in the Spanish room leaked like a bloody sieve all over the equally new carpet. Spanish is now held in the typing room. The landscapers want $400 per tree to plant our gift oak trees, and the janitor quit.

Next week is Parents Night. We have a guest speaker. Ann Gordon from NAES will visit Galveston for the first time. She was to stay with me and I had hoped that things would

100

be in pristine order. The painter informs me that he will not be finished with the house.

Intrepidly, I trudged my two miles today, proceeded to hose myself off and get dressed for dinner. I thought I looked ravishing. I must have just looked ravished. The waiter, blessedly, did not start with me. Around the table my old buddy and former Board President said, "I'll have two scotch and waters."

"A double?" the waiter asked.

"No. Two. One for me and one for the Headmistress." It's not my fault, world. I didn't order it. I only drank it to be nice. Mama always said to take what is offered you. I wonder why that waiter looked so much like a St. Bernard?

You know, with enough understanding friends I might survive October after all.

P. S. I have been inundated with box tops. Thank you for your interest.

20

M Y FRIEND GWEN BROUGHT ME A BOOK EN-
TITLED *ELVIS IS DEAD AND I DON'T FEEL SO
GOOD MYSELF.* I'D SAY THAT SUMS IT UP NICELY
SINCE I'M CHORTLING OVER THAT TITLE WHILE FLAT ON
MY BACK IN ST. MARY'S HOSPITAL FOLLOWING HASTY
AND UNFORESEEN ABDOMINAL SURGERY.

 I know what you heard but it's an overstatement of
fact. I did *not* get so incensed upon reading the last "Hickory
Stick" that I literally — in the vernacular of the street —
busted a gut. I was a little surprised to find paragraph six
the lead paragraph and my trumpets and tympani closing
lollygagging around in the middle of the column. I accepted
it with characteristic equanimity and soothed my soul by re-
reading a fan letter from a Houston gentleman. True fanship
is writing a letter on a column only a mother could love.

 Remember when I told you Rotten Russell, Boy
Board President, had to go? Well, this time I really mean it.
When called and told that surgery had been performed to
remove my gall bladder and wasn't that a surprise? Russell
said it didn't surprise him. I quote his immortal words di-
rectly. "The surprise is that anybody with that much gall isn't
solidified all over." If he hadn't just created a winter green-
house for me and bought me my own electric staple gun,
he'd go. He'd go by Tuesday. I'm only putting up with him
until I get a little better.

 I'm getting better daily and that's how I had so much
time to study the newspaper this morning. I found three
articles on facing pages that cry for comment. One is an
editorial, one is on the University of Texas survey on basic

102

skills for entering freshmen, and one is an announcement of the opening of a college for dyslexics.

Let me take the survey first. I quote: "Even the most talented and gifted students from high school across the nation can no longer perform basic academic skills that were common a decade ago."

Hogwash! Define "talented and gifted students." If you define a talented and gifted student as anyone who made A's in homemaking in the Greater Tuna Consolidated School District, then that probably figures, but it's a rather loose way to run a survey. I don't know who picked the sample but I assure you there are students in St. Stephen's and Episcopal High and TMI, to name a few of our Episcopal schools, who are as well as or better prepared than ours were a decade ago. And there are plenty of them. It's the result of having standards and sticking to them. They get those well-prepared students from Trinity and St. Andrew's and St. Francis and the rest because we, too, have standards and stick to them.

The next deathless comment concerns colleges with remedial courses. "Now even Harvard has remedial courses," it says. Why in life should Harvard, with fifty applications for every place and enough money per student to burn a wet mule, bother with remedial courses? Try these: (a) Greed and Avarice; (b) Do-Goodership; (c) Government Requirements; (d) All of the Above.

The government requires a certain number of minority students or you can't get government grants. The Minority Student category has been broadened to include all colors just so long as they are unprepared. Grants supplement salaries; ergo, professors will put up with the remedial hassle to get the money. Check (a) for Greed and Avarice.

"Big" and "rich" are adjectives that some universities seem to think are generally necessary to salvation. What possible good does it do to be big, rich, and turn out

103

uneducated products? Big and rich are the two main ingre-
dients for perpetuating a bureaucracy. The bigger it is the
harder the parasites are to locate and the richer it is the less
pressing the demand to locate them. That's the core of it
but it's festooned in clouds of smoke that spell, "Reach out
to your fellow man, give him your hand, and pull him up to
your level."

Let's leap to the next article for a minute, entitled,
"A College for Dyslexics." Dyslexia simply means a reading
dysfunction. It's a trash term. It's about as definitive as
"tummy ache." There are an infinite number of causes —
some more easily cured than others. I was dyslexic. So were
my brother and cousin, along with some really heavyweights
like Nelson Rockefeller and Edison and Hans Christian
Anderson and probably Einstein. We worked out of it in a
normal classroom situation because that's what people did.
It was part of going to school. Some cases are hard core.
They don't re-route that easily. These people used to choose
some way to make a living that didn't require advanced skills
in reading. The result was that we had skilled artisans in
wood and metal, magnificent chefs, artists, and there were
dreamers and planners in every field. They took pride in
their work and realized that education has nothing to do
with college degrees. Dyslexics are problem solvers. They
have to be.

Somebody convinced parents that each child had to
have a college degree. I don't know who it was but there
ought to be a special place in hell for him. Those degrees
are frightfully expensive and totally worthless. Two quotes:
first, concerning Dyslexic U., "It will cost $17,000 *more* than
Harvard or M.I.T."

The next concerns D.U. and other schools with dyslexia programs. They name specifically Southern Illinois.
"These people provide ways to 'get around' the handicap.
They include student scribes to take lecture notes and help
write term papers and oral exams with no time limit."

I remember the old days when such a program existed at my alma mater. It was called "cheating."

Scenario I: Johnny-Can't-Read has a rich daddy who spends $17,000 more than Harvard to get a piece of sheepskin for J.C.R. J.C.R. goes to the work-a-day world via daddy's company and lives happily ever after. It's okay with me. I'm just going to pick up the Brooklyn Bridge and drop in on old dad for a business chat.

Scenario II: Same problem. No rich daddy. Parent quote: "Cost is a factor but you just scrape together every penny you have. If your child needed a heart transplant you'd do it. There's no difference." Wrong, lady, there is no similarity. Dyslexia is not terminal and your expensive remedy is flagrantly snake oil. Do you suppose the boss of Big Company of America is going to give unlimited time for his reports to be in, accept them orally, or provide and pay a scribe to write them for some dyslexic employee? It makes no sense at all.

Education costs a bloody fortune. The reason it does is because we're buying a flaming bunco scam. To cut the cost of college education, take only qualified students in college. That cuts size which cuts costs and extra programs. It also eliminates parasites who feed off those who dream of unattainable goals for their children.

Everybody needs to be able to swim to the side of the pool so he won't drown. Some people enjoy it and master a degree of swimming that affords them pleasure all their lives. There is nothing chiseled in stone anywhere that says it's everyone's God-given right to win an Olympic swimming medal — or a university degree. Parents, wise up.

21

MY ALARM WENT FRITZY THIS MORNING. JUST TWO PIROUETTES AND OUT IT GOES. REASON UNKNOWN. IT DIDN'T MUCH MATTER BECAUSE IT WAS SUNDAY AND I HAD A COUPLE OF HOURS TO LOLL AROUND ANYWAY. TOMORROW, INEVITABLY, IS MONDAY AND IT MAKES A DIFFERENCE.

I called My-Faithful-Secretary-Tonto to apprise her of this malfunction in my routine and she allowed as how she couldn't possibly get a substitute for me at this hour and she would call me when it was time to get up if she got around to it. I think she is a closet Redskin fan having a fit of pique. I didn't protest. The result, however, is that there is no alternative for me but to sit around awake and wait for it to be time to go to school. One would think that the boss would have certain prerogatives, but I think the answer is that it's not my turn to be boss this week.

That happens to headmistresses periodically. It's sort of passive resistance. Gandhi would have loved it. Here and now I step to the podium to clearly state that it simply isn't our fault. It's the fault of Julius Caesar, or whoever set up the calendar the last time. January is budget time, recruitment time, fund-raising time, calendar-planning time, and, if you have been honored with an invitation to be on an accreditation team, it is accrediting time. That leaves little or no time for mundane school things even if your pipes didn't break in the freeze, and mine did. Teachers are a lot like children, or wives and husbands, or mothers and fathers. They want their share of the time. Certainly they should have it, but where is it supposed to come from? They could take it out of my share, except I ran out of share about last Tuesday.

Two weeks ago it was a little fund-raising event in Dallas that took a full day of my time. This week it was a meeting with TEA in Austin concerning new accreditation procedures. Next week it is the SAES board meeting in San Antonio. The first really shouldn't take your time, and the last hasn't yet occurred, so let me regale you with the middle one. It'll salve my conscience about being out of the tent.

Prior to this time the Texas Education Agency has accredited private and parochial schools on a basis that compared unfavorably with a crap shoot in Las Vegas. One applied, had the proper number of grades, filled out the proper papers and discovered that the rules applied to everyone except, of course, for the ones from which you were about to be excused. These depended mainly on who did the accrediting. There were no set rules. If the accreditor wished you to have vocational training in your school, it became important for you to do so. If they wanted your teachers to be certified in the State of Texas, I suppose you had to do that. They just never did require that. They had the power to waive many things.

Things are now changing. First we heard that private schools would no longer be accredited. That appears at this time to be a fallacy. There is a new bill in the House which we all expect to be passed in March. It is called House Bill 246. It lays out the number of courses to be taught, what will be taught in them, and how one will judge when that teaching has been done successfully.

The question was, how does this affect our schools? In an unprecedented move, the TEA invited private schools to be present for a discussion of the problems and consequences. We were. It was a very nice turn-out. I saw everybody from SAES and from independent schools and a lot of people I haven't met yet. The TEA bunch assured us that nothing would be done to us in the middle of the night

107

without prior notice of their intentions. That was consoling. They stated that when the bill was passed our schools would no longer be exempted by whim. Sets of rules would be written that would exempt certain schools from certain things that were deemed inappropriate for these schools, and that the rest of the rules would be strictly enforced.

The one thing that they would not speak to was the certification of teachers. It is the one thing that I find most disturbing. It does not bother me to have the prescribed number of days of teaching. We always have. Nor does it bother me to teach the prescribed number of minutes per day for certain subjects. I wouldn't make the same diagnosis of the necessary, but it doesn't ruin my whole day. The thing that does bother me is the certification of teachers.

I have found that the certification of a teacher as having the correct number of hours of education to teach in the State of Texas has about as much relation to their ability to teach as bull-fighting has to agriculture. Teaching is a gift. As long as one has a grasp of the subject to be taught and the innate gift for teaching, things are going to come out okay. I don't need the State to tell me when that is happening — or not happening. Public education has fallen under the pall of criticism recently and I would point out that it happened under the auspices of certified teachers. Some are excellent. Some should have stayed home. It is an area I worry about and will, undoubtedly, speak to at a later date.

22

"I BUY YOU THE BOOK. I SEND YOU TO SCHOOL, AND ALL YOU DO IS CHEW ON THE COVER!" I'VE HEARD THAT PHRASE SINCE EARLY CHILD-HOOD. IT FOLLOWS SEVERE ATTACKS OF THE STUPIDS AND IS MOST OFTEN HEARD DURING PITCH GAMES AND WHEN ONE HAS LED FROM A KING. WITHOUT EXCEP-TION IT IS UTTERED BY THE HAPLESS PARTNER IN THIS CARD-PLAYING VENTURE.

You can tell that it comes from a bygone era from the simple assumption that the inside of the book is more enlightening and intellectually nourishing than the cover. Alas! It used to be true. That, of course, was before we got readability formulas. Readability formulas are those scales used to determine the level of difficulty of a basal reader. It assigns certain values to words. Two-syllable words get more points than one-syllable words. Three-syllable words are be-yond the pale. Analyzing a text according to a readability formula involves counting and averaging syllables in words and words in sentences. When one does that, and factors in the hard words — "hard" being defined by the text maker — then you have a readability score. Many states, Texas in-cluded, require that textbooks purchased be appropriate to the grade level as determined by readability scores.

Readability formulas were first applied in the twen-ties with the perfectly respectable intent of matching the material to the ability of the reader. Like a good number of other things in the education field, it has progressed to a state of absurdity. I throw in Exhibit A. These examples of basal readings for young children based on readability formulas are quoted by Georgia M. Green in a chapter entitled, "On the Appropriateness of Adaptation in Primary Level Basal Readers," from *Learning to Read in American Schools,* edited by Richard C. Anderson, Jean Osborn, and Robert J. Tierney. I found them quoted in the February edition of "Basic Education."

THE TORTOISE AND THE HARE

Rabbit said, "I can run. I can run fast. You can't run fast."

Turtle said, "Look, Rabbit. See the park. You and I will run to the park."

Rabbit said, "I want to stop. I'll stop here. I can run, but Turtle can't. I can get to the park fast."

Turtle said, "I can't run fast. But I will not stop. Rabbit can't see me. I'll get to the park."

Not only does the basal reader version present us with a story both boring and jerky, it is also incomplete, inaccurate and does not follow the formula for a fable. In fact, it makes no sense at all. Can you tell from this story that there was a race between the Tortoise and the Hare? Can you tell who won? The definition of a fable is that the story must have a moral. Is there any discernable moral to this story? Does winning through perseverance *ever* come through in this story? Whoever wrote it ought to be put in jail

THE SHOEMAKER AND THE ELVES

Tap, tap, tap. See me work. I make good things. See the red ones. See the blue ones. See the yellow ones. No, no, no. I do not want red ones. I do not want blue ones. I want green ones.

No, no, no. I do not want big ones. I want little ones.

No, no, no. I do not want little ones. I want big ones.

Oh, my. Oh, my. No one wants my things. I will go to bed. I will work in the morning.

Remember the story of the Shoemaker and the Elves? The shoemaker went to bed exhausted but unfinished with his task and the elves came during the night and made shoes for him so that he waked up to a task completed. I'm not sure what the moral to that one is. I have never had elves finish any work for me. However, this story doesn't bill itself as a fable. It is called a fairy story. Without impugning the elves, I'd say that's true. Does anyone ever mention elves in the basal reader version? Does it say anything about shoes being made during the night? Does it, in fact, say anything *at all?*

You wonder why Johnny can't read? In order for a child to learn to read he has to have something to read that makes sense. This literary creation is one notch below Jabberwocky in the gibberish sweepstakes.

This morning the *Houston Post* ran a feature called "Why John Can't Read." I won't quote the story to you, but the point is well taken. Not only can't Johnny read, Papa is having some difficulty puzzling out all the words also. Presumably he was born after the 1920 readability formula came into being. Let me tell you what John, Sr., grandpapa, cut his reading teeth on. I refer to the McGuffey Reader. This is an excerpt from the first-grade book of John, Sr. It concerns making a bird nest.

"How does a bird make a nest so strong, Willie?"

"The mother bird has her bill and claws to work with, but she would not know how to make the nest if God did not teach her. Do you see what it is made of?"

"Yes, Willie, I see some horse hairs and some dry grass."

I tried to figure that according to the acceptable readability formula and it ran right off the scale, but it is much easier reading than that other drivel because it makes sense.

111

The sixth-grade reader for McGuffey contains things I didn't read until high school and a couple I didn't hit until college. It has the address of Henry V to his troops. You know, the one that begins,

Once more into the breach, dear friends, once more:
Or close the wall up with our British dead.

I never did read that. I saw it down at the Paramount picture show when Laurence Olivier played. It would have been nice to have at least heard about Henry V before I bought the popcorn. McGuffey's also has "Thanatopsis" and the church scene from "Evangeline." It's called *McGuffey's Eclectic Reader*, and indeed it is.

There's not a lot I can do about textbooks. Ranting and raving is good for the spleen but has little or no effect on education. However, I do see the cavalry coming over the hill. The McGuffey has been reprinted and I have located them. Through the generosity of a donor I have managed to raise $1,600, which is the price it takes to place a McGuffey in the hands of every kid at Trinity School. It is in the process of being done.

Another old saying I grew up with is, "It takes three generations from shirt-sleeves to shirt-sleeves." It was supposed to outline the economic law for redistribution of money — or the ineptitude of heirs. Perhaps the converse will be equivalent. Perhaps, with prayer, fasting and the McGuffey it will take three generations from literacy to literacy. I fervently hope so.

23

PLEASE WALK BY ME QUIETLY AND DON'T DROP ANYTHING. I'M CONCENTRATING. I'VE GOT A RESEARCH PROJECT DUE IN TWO WEEKS AND I HAVEN'T READ ALL THE BOOKS YET.

It seems that I contracted in June to make the Texas Independence Day speech to the Daughters of the Republic of Texas on the Fall of the Alamo. Unfortunately, my knowledge of the fall of the Alamo is bounded on the north by a fourth-grade field trip and on the south by John Wayne. I have, however, returned to the scene since then. Last year I judged the Battle of Flowers Parade. The judges' stand was in front of the Alamo. We didn't get in. The TMI boys were guarding it. You don't get by those TMI boys. They are from an Episcopal school.

Included in the history of San Antonio, over which I have pored, is an account of the first diocesan council of the Missionary Diocese of West Texas. In 1875, Texas was still pretty sparsely populated. The Missionary Diocese of West Texas was composed of 110,000 square miles of frontier with seven clergy and 427 communicants. Yet when the 34-year-old missionary bishop, Robert Woodward Barnward Elliot, stood up to address the first convocation of the diocese, it was not the privations of travel on the frontier that he addressed. The most desperate need that he perceived was the lack of schools.

"I should feel that the church was moving onward with certainty and precision, secure in her future, if I could tell you that she was furnished with schools where the generation that will succeed us was receiving the refining, conservative and Godly training which her education imparts . . ."

The 133rd Diocesan Council of the Diocese of Texas met recently. Until a few short years ago there was still no canon in this diocese requesting schools or even recognizing that they existed. I wrote one. Knowing that it was going to be whittled to a toothpick, I added more ruffles than a flamenco costume. Everybody had to pledge allegiance to the Southwestern Association of Episcopal Schools and make me Mother Superior of the entire Western World in perpetuity. The hope was that when the whittling began it would be this fluff that got shaved and the good stuff would survive. However, if the committee wished to let it stand in all its pristine purity, I had my coronation dress pressed. I never needed it, but a canon did get passed that recognized that the church did have schools in the Diocese of Texas and that these schools played an important part in the life of the church. It set up a Diocesan Committee on Schools. I serve.

I was manning the booth for Episcopal Day Schools at Council. I had the graveyard shift since everyone was in eating and listening to the Friday speaker, but I was not bored. I bought a cookbook from the Cathedral Ladies and had worked my way down to Oysters Alberta before I had my first customer. He only had one question. In a puzzled tone he asked, "What are you-all doing here?"

The Mouth of the Guadalupe is rarely caught speechless, but this one stymied me. I stammered that we were a vital part of the church mission and as such had the duty to be represented at council. Repartee is what you wish you'd said. Few of us have a second chance. That's why I bless *The Texas Churchman* daily in the same breath with Mama and Trinity School.

The questioner probably doesn't read the "Hickory Stick," but I'm going to give it a try anyway. OKAY, OUT THERE, MAN-IN-THE-GREY-COAT-THAT-WASN'T-LISTENING-TO-THE-SPEAKER, THIS IS WHY WE ARE HERE.

The Diocese of Texas has 49 schools educating 7,291 students in the highest academic traditions, and in the faith of the Church. Our diocese has almost 7% of all the Episcopal schools in the country. We employ 613 teachers at a median salary of $10,000. Chapel services range in number per week from one to five, which is no small evangelistic effort since only about 20% of the students in Episcopal schools are baptized Episcopalians.

And that, Sir, is why Episcopal schools had a booth at Council. As Hogan used to say to Snead, "You're away, Sam."

24

REMEMBER THE CHINESE YEAR OF THE OX? THIS IS THE YEAR OF WHOSE OX — AS IN WHOSE-OX-GOT-GORED. AS A PRACTICAL MATTER, EVERY END OF MAY IS THE TIME OF WHOSE OX. NO DOUBT YOU IN SCHOOLS HAVE NOTICED THAT.

Each year at this time we hold Honors Day to extol our own for their many triumphs in whatever field. As the old rhyme goes, "Some can sing, and some can dance, and some can play croquet." We praise them all for whatever their talent.

We follow that with a magnificent Commencement — full dress — with 300 children enthusiastically singing "Evensong," and pipers, and as many bishops as we can muster — all walking around in their red dresses getting hugged. It's a glorious night. Bishops, banners and tympani. It's the formula for a memorable Commencement.

Remember when your mama told you to watch your celebration 'cause there was always a morning after? They even immortalized it in song. Everybody's right. There is.

There's that next morning when the cookie crumbs crunch underfoot and the altar flowers are beginning to shed on the hall carpet, and you walk in the office with head down contemplating the book orders for next year, and how much it's going to cost to paint classrooms, and whether you really can afford to strip and refinish fifty kindergarten chairs suffering from twenty years of cheap paint, or whether it is wiser and nobler to order plastic chairs which will crack in two years. And there waits your reception committee — the Mothers' Mafia.

116

In groups of one or two, in 1/2- or 3/4-hour segments you are regaled with their advice on improving the whole procedure. They have come to give you input. It runs thusly:
Honors' Day could be vastly improved IF:
A. There were more emphasis on academics and less on extracurricular activities.
B. There were less emphasis on academics and more on extracurricular activities.
C. There were less music.
D. There were more music.
E. There were more input from the parents' organization.
F. We had fewer people trying to run our show.

It all depends, you see, on whose ox got gored.

And that, my dear, is when headmistresses go to China. They can hardly find you in China, particularly if you're headed for Xian — to the tombs. Telephone service is terrible there.

The far corners of the world where one can hide are becoming scarcer, but if you're inventive you can manage. I formed my own tour company. If you've got your own tour company you can usually wrangle a ticket. I keep a valid passport as an article of faith. Once each year — right after the annual convention of the Mothers' Mafia — I gather my friends around me and we all go to — wherever. It costs about the same as therapy and it's much more fun. This year I'm taking the Board President as insurance.

Funny thing. When you get back and really start gearing up for September, it's all forgotten, and the year begins on the same upbeat as Commencement. I think that's why God endorsed vacations. Happy summer.

117

25

I'M HOME, MOM. CHINA WAS A REVELATION AND A DELIGHT, NOT TO MENTION A SHOPPER'S PARADISE. BUT THAT'S ALL BEHIND ME NOW — AS IS ABOUT FIVE POUNDS THAT SEEMS TO BE RESIDING COMFORTABLY BEHIND ME ALSO. HOW COME MOST FOLK LOSE WEIGHT IN CHINA AND I DON'T?

Anyway, I'm home and back with mundane and magnificent delights of summertime in the USA. I would love to have absorbed some of the inscrutable oriental insights into man's state of being while I was traveling, but alas, I returned with the same pragmatic mindset with which I departed.

I tried. I read Zen. I attended a Buddhist service. I learned all about the yin and the yang. I really thought I might be making some progress. Then I returned to watch a grandfather of my acquaintance attempting to teach his grandson to swim. I knew right off that philosophically I had blown five grand and three weeks.

The swimmer's grandfather was imparting his erudite engineering best. He traced the theory of water displacement and buoyancy. He explained the theory of arm and leg motion and how it fit into the great overall swimming picture. The kid looked blank and staunchly refused to take his feet off the bottom.

Who can blame him? Who, in their right mind, gives a big kazoo about Archimedes when it's deep out there and your chances of getting back to shore are slim and none.

Some teachers can't keep their mouths shut and I am president of that sorority. "Never mind Archimedes," said I. "Put your head down in the water and blow bubbles. When you run out of air raise up and get some more. Kick your feet and swing your arms and pretty soon you'll get where you are going. When you can either touch bottom or feel safe enough so you don't care, *then* we'll discuss buoyancy and Archimedes and naval architecture."

Some great educators try valiantly to put the cart before the horse. There are some advantages to this. Those of us who have spent some time with the horse in front know that there are certain discomforts thereto appertaining, but there seem to be very few alternatives educationally.

I point as Exhibit A to modern math. That was the cart before the horse in spades. If you already knew math and accepted the patterns and structures, then modern math was just as plain as the nose on somebody's face. If, however, you harbored some reservation about two and two really always making four, then perhaps Boolean algebra might not be the next logical step for, say, second grade.

I don't expound this theory simply sitting contentedly on five pounds acquired in Xian, China. I spent a year teaching geometry to first graders in Tallahassee, Florida, under the direction of Dr. Eugene V. Nichols of modern math fame. First graders learned it okay. They got from Point A to Point B just fine and learned about the infinite number of points in between. They weren't too good on theory. They thought Pythagoras was a choo-choo train. Why not? It goes from one point to another passing all the points in between.

I'm preparing for next year at the moment by replacing carpet and counting books and making schedules. I do hope I remember to remind teachers to forget about Archimedes for the first couple of years. Just tell the kids to put their heads down, kick their feet, flay their arms, and trust us. They'll swim through the year just fine. If they begin to go under we are there to hold them up. When they are big enough to swim the Channel, then they can worry about Pythagoras and Archimedes. When I reach an equal state I plan to start worrying about Zen.

119

26

I STAYED DURING THE STORM. FURTHERMORE, I STAYED ALONE. BEFORE YOU CONCLUDE THAT I AM (A) INSANE, (B) A RECLUSE, (C) A PARIAH, (D) ALL OF THE ABOVE, LET ME ASSURE YOU THAT I HAD SEVERAL INVITATIONS — ALL OF THEM ATTRACTIVE — AND HAD I NOT DECIDED TO STAND STAUNCHLY TO PROTECT SCHOOL AND HOME I WOULD HAVE HIGHTAILED IT DOWN IH 10 TO OLE TARA TO SIP JULEPS AND WATCH THE TV COVERAGE LIKE OTHER INTELLIGENT FOLK.

I was prepared to protect. I was a sentinel of security. I had everything but a shotgun over my knees. I was a bulwark — until the lights went out.

There are not too many things one can do when the lights go out, and for one alone even those choices are limited. I weighed my alternatives in the balance and found the best of the lot was to go to sleep.

Sleeping through one of the five worst hurricanes of the century is insensitive if not downright boorish, but what's a headmistress to do? TV is off. The lights are out. School opens shortly and one might as well be rested for it.

So I slept. Soundly. True, I did awaken about the time a large crash shattered what should have been silence. I complained to an unlistening world that this was one noisy storm and should show more consideration for those of us asleep.

It had shown some consideration. The crash was a large palm tree falling on my fence. Three inches closer and it would have gotten my house. Three feet closer and it would have gotten me. Ignorance is bliss — to coin a phrase.

Eight-thirty A.M. Phone rings, waking me up. How were things? They were fine, said I. Nothing to it. Like shooting fish in a barrel, said I, faking it all the way.

I wandered in to get my coffee and noticed that my fence had blown down, the roofs of half of Surfside resided in my front yard, and my patio roof had decided to find another habitation. I was embarrassed to call back and retract.

The winds died down and the faithful began arriving for a health and welfare check-up. I prevailed on family to take me to school to survey the damage there.

The school had been petted past its usual summer sprucing this year. Rooms had been painted, carpet replaced and fences fixed. We were pristine pretty. There was, however, one exception. Among the property owned by Trinity is an ugly corner I have been trying to reclaim all year. It was acquired during the expansion and has not been renovated because we ran out of money. It began life as a Mobil filling station and progressed to the Busy Bee Cab Company. To say it is an eyesore is to endow it with an elegance undeserved. All year I have been trying to get it painted. My building committee allowed as how paint ain't cheap and soon as we decide what we want to do with the property we are going to tear it down anyway. My pleas for urban renewal have not prevailed.

In my few waking moments during the night I sent up the prayer, "Lord, protect Trinity School except, of course, for the Busy Bee."

I arrived to discover water on the new carpet, 4,000 feet of decimated fence, stains on the fresh paint, and the Busy Bee standing like Gibraltar.

The storm has passed. Slowly we return to normal. Phones have begun to ring and air-conditioning has finally returned to Tern Street. Reflecting on the week's events I discover two home truths. (1) I am undaunted by danger but I detest inconvenience and do not suffer it well, and (2) it's time to think about writing the fall chapel lectures. It's more appetizing to contemplate a short, invigorating and convenient hurricane.

121

27

I'M PLANNING THE THANKSGIVING PROGRAM. BASI-
CALLY IT DOESN'T TAKE MUCH PLANNING BECAUSE
WE'VE BEEN DOING THE SAME THING SINCE THE
MIND OF MAN RUNNETH NOT TO THE CONTRARY. EV-
ERYBODY BRINGS A NON-PERISHABLE FOOD ITEM AND
PRESENTS IT AT THE ALTAR AS A TOKEN SHARING OF
GOD'S BOUNTY AT THIS HARVEST TIME. IT'S KIND OF
FADDY NOW THAT FOLK ARE MAKING RECORDS FOR RE-
LIEF IN AFRICA. THE FACT IS THAT HUNGER HAS BEEN
AMONG US LOCALLY SINCE BEFORE IT WAS FASHIONABLE
AND THAT FACT NEEDED TO BE ADDRESSED TANGIBLY.
WE'VE DONE OUR THING FOR SIXTEEN YEARS THAT I
KNOW OF, AND I INHERITED THE PROGRAM. WITH ALL
THE PUBLICITY WE SHOULD RECEIVE A BETTER RETURN.
ST. VINCENT'S HOUSE CAN USE IT, ALFREDA ASSURES ME.

There are, however, things that occur at this time of
year, equally fashionable, for which I am not so thankful. I
refer specifically to today's National Smoke-Out.

I have smoked — and still do on occasion — but I
don't smoke at school and I object strenuously to the school
smelling like smoke. It's not a wholesome atmosphere and
I have voiced this sentiment from time to time — like every
morning. I have bought air filters for the lounge and office
and muttered ominously about folk trashing up my office. I
am ignored totally and regally.

Today, on the Great Smoke-Out, the offenders decided to shape up — with the following result.

I arrived at my office at the usual time and prepared
for chapel. I began the versicles.

"What are the hymns today?" I asked in my usual absent-minded way. "280 and 566," my secretary snapped like I'd accused her of spitting on the flag. I went to chapel to pray for her smoke-filled soul. I returned in due time after trooping the color around the school just to let everybody know I was back in town. "You certainly preached a long time today," was my accusatory greeting. "It's 9:15." I refrained from pointing out that I was the one who owned the time clock, not the one who punched it. I retired to my office to write a Middle School curriculum brochure. I have a new word processor and it's quieter than a typewriter. I thought I might quietly hide until the day was over.

Not so. Apropos of nothing, an irate secretary stormed my office armed with Webster's forty-pound dictionary open halfway, and, shaking it ominously over my head, pronounced between clenched teeth, "I'm going to teach this to you if it's the last thing I do. 'Renown' has a past tense and you have used it wrong *again! See?*" The offending object was my travel brochure which has no relation to Trinity School. I accepted the rebuke with grace and pointed out that there were other typos in the brochure as well. The printer remained absolved and all errors of syntax in the civilized Western World were laid at my door in alphabetical order.

Lunch is a sort of social season with us daily. It takes place in my office whether I'm ready or not. I knew today was not auspicious so I arranged to take a donor to lunch, feeling smug at my advanced planning. Lo, I did not depart in time. While I was trying diligently to work I was interrupted by plaintive cries of "This is awful! Who's got the gum?", and other terse statements appropriate to the day.

I survived. I found committee meetings to attend, classes to teach and errands to run. I picked up typewriters

123

for the teacher's lounge. I even went to the Lower School basketball game. Their new uniforms were lovely. Ipecac would have been lovely compared to living in my office.

This may be the start of something big. They may all shuck the habit. It's probably six, two, and even they won't. In either case, today I'm not thankful for the Great American Smoke-Out. It was a character-building experience for me in a manner totally unexpected.

Next year if they have a Smoke-Out I'm going to hunt down the sonovagun who thought it up and present him with a present — in fact, three presents — and they all work for me! Smoke-Outs are a great idea and he deserves all the rights and privileges thereto appertaining — including putting up with all the confirmed and addicted smokers paying oh so vociferous lip service to his cause. As I gift him with this trio, I won't be able to resist saying it. Have a good day.

28

I T'S A LINE I STOLE FROM FIESTA CORONATION IN SAN ANTONIO. THEY ALWAYS BEGIN THE FESTIVITIES BY SAYING, "EACH RECURRING SPRINGTIME . . ." IT FITS LOTS OF OCCASIONS. TAKE, FOR INSTANCE, ACADEMY AWARDS NIGHT. EACH RECURRING SPRINGTIME . . . EVERYONE AGREES THAT FOR BANAL AND BORING, THE ACADEMY AWARDS HAVE NO PEER, BUT OFTEN I FIND MYSELF GRIPING AND WATCHING. I WATCHED PART OF THE SHOW THIS TIME. SERVES ME RIGHT.

I mourned because there were no heroes. I miss 'em. I used to spend every Saturday afternoon in the company of the neighborhood bund savoring a Halloway's Black Cow and watching Hoppy, Gene and Roy do right. Flash Gordon always bested Ming from Mongo and Buster Crabbe always out-swam the alligators. The Super-Marvel men fought crime and evil, and even Joan Crawford and Bette Davis weren't allowed to sin and go scot-free. Well, mostly they weren't. Sometimes, for artistic purposes, they just walked out into the ocean and the curtain closed without telling us whether or not they could swim.

On this occasion, Barbara Walters interviewed three nominees for best actress. They are our present-day heroines, rich and famous, to be admired and copied by our young. One was expecting an illegitimate child. She spoke of it freely. One was herself illegitimate and described her promiscuous youth and her incestuous childhood. The other has devoted years to flouting convention. She may have a couple of what Maybelle used to call "illimates," too. Sounded like it.

One played an obsessed sexual deviate, one a widow who was having an affair with her fiancé's brother and the third played a much abused femme sole attacked in her own home — or so it seemed from the film clip. How's that array for role models for our children? Just your garden variety girl next door.

This prime-time gala followed a program decrying teenage pregnancy and child abuse and demanding of educators that they do a better job teaching not only math but morals to our children. The disingenuousness of the media is appalling!

They got Jimmy Swaggert for undisclosed crimes against humanity that, from the carefully dropped clues, would seem to be voyeurism. I don't know how they're going to make that one stick. All you have to do to be a voyeur these days is turn on the tube. Makes a lot of sense, doesn't it?

I didn't stick around to see who won. I knew I wouldn't approve. I bet on Custer against the Indians every time. I hoped it was "The Last Emperor." It was a pretty show. These sweaty T-shirt stories bore me witless. The Emperor, at least, allowed as how opium ruined his country, which was a mark for morality, but then went off to collaborate with the enemy. Big hero.

Did you notice how many of the actors thanked their mother? Motherhood doesn't have to share top billing if you don't know who your father is.

How are educators supposed to combat that? In six hours we are expected to teach reading, spelling, math, science, history and morals. The next six hours you have a steady stream of immorals — or amorals.

I'm sick to death of education being the whipping boy of a nation cheered on by a media sinking in slime and violence. Clean up your own act, media, and when you're willing to help in the battle to educate a moral generation, come back and talk to me. Otherwise, collect your exorbitant salaries and shut up.

29

EVERY FRAZZLING YEAR IT'S SOMETHING. AS MILTON BERLE IS REPORTED TO HAVE SAID, "I GOT MY NOSE FIXED AND NOW MY MOUTH WON'T WORK."

Struggling to get school open, as I do every August, I'm visited by the plagues of Egypt, as I seem to be every August. Last year it was Hurricane Alicia. We survived that and, as a reward for valor, this year we get Marvin Zindler. Neither one was fatal — or even terribly debilitating — but each in its own way was among the world's larger nuisances. It's the timing that is so obnoxious. Why, Lord, just before school starts? I must have spent an extra twenty hours on the phone.

Hurricane Alicia proved to be of great benefit to Trinity School. Without it, TES would have taken ten years to get the physical plant in such pristine shape. Perhaps the Zindler Caper will prove as beneficial — said Pollyanna The Glad Girl.

I did not always face this happening with such equanimity. In fact, this is the fourth edition of the August "Hickory Stick." The first two Tonto refused to type. Said it simply wasn't fitting for a headmistress to speak thusly — and a Hockaday girl to boot. The third edition I sneaked off to type and mail myself. *The Texas Churchman* declined to run it.

Undoubtedly that showed rare good judgement, but it is a pity. Mark Twain complained one time that in the use of inelegant language his wife knew all the words but she couldn't get the tune. I do not suffer from the same linguistic inadequacy. My pony, Ole Butterbean, used to reside at

Mr. Edgar Lannom's Mule Barn, and while waiting for her to be saddled I had an elegant sufficiency of language lessons from the Mule Skinner's Manual. On occasion I am eloquent, and I considered the recent Zindler episode a suitable occasion. A great piece of literature remains unpublished but it may not be lost to you forever. For two box tops and a self-addressed stamped envelope, you, too, may receive an unabridged version.

I do hate to be caught off guard. I wasn't even in the ring, bobbing and weaving. I was sitting in front of the tube watching the Olympics and eating a sardine sandwich. Here came Channel 13 News featuring Mad Marvin and Trinity Episcopal School.

How in life could I have remained unaware, you wonder? Easy. Nobody ever contacted me. The complainant called while school was closed for vacation and talked to the bookkeeper who just happened to be in checking the mail. Bookkeepers are not in charge of re-writing policy and ours didn't attempt to. She pointed out that the parent had a signed contract and that bookkeepers were not empowered to release folk from contracts and refund money. School would be open again on Monday and perhaps she'd like to come in then and discuss it. It wasn't much different from a dozen other such calls.

She didn't come in on Monday nor did she call. Neither did Zindler.

Now I don't mean to imply that things might have been different had the parent talked to me. Had both of them come with a brass band and firecrackers I wouldn't have returned a nickel. Schools can't do business betting on the come. Ours is a standard contract used by every school and camp extant. You pay to secure a place and the school hires teachers and buys books on the basis of that assurance. We've been to court three times to test it and won all three. The more entertaining ones I have chronicled in previous "Hickory Sticks." I even received a donation to the

Headmistress's Bail Fund as the result of one of them. We did not even suggest that she pay the remaining 80% of the tuition which she legally owes. All of which would have been explained ad nauseam had anyone bothered to inquire.

I just simply do not like my business being handled by three hundred other people. Did you place a bet that I might have voiced that sentiment? Pay the man. Within seconds of recovering from the seizure with the sardine sandwich I was on the line. Within the hour I had spoken to the rector, the executive committee of the school board, the attorneys, two bishops, one canon, and assorted priests and deacons. They didn't think headmistresses knew those words either.

Shall I take on Channel 13 *and* Mr. Z toe-to-toe? I'd dearly love to. I'd lose thirty pounds and call Adele Simpson for a fitting. If Miss Rosalie Hoff were still living I'd take elocution lessons again. The sad and simple fact is that you can't beat the media because the media cheats. Ask General Westmoreland. I could win every round in real life and it wouldn't show that way after expedient editing. As Exhibit A I give you Channel 13's recent reminiscence of Hurricane Alicia. To the best of my memory they said:

"Hurricane Alicia hit Galveston Island one year ago today, killing 21 people. It was the worst disaster ever to have hit the island."

Last time I heard, Alicia took no lives. Even if 21 people expired before January 1 and blamed it on the effects of that hurricane, those 6,000 people who died in the 1900 storm are going to be pretty surprised to find that Alicia was the worst disaster ever to hit the Island. But Channel 13 came pretty close to getting the day right. I guess that's about as much as you can hope for from the media.

129

30

I SPENT PART OF THIS MORNING TUTORING A YOUNG LADY WHO FINDS FRACTIONS TO BE ILLEGAL, IMMORAL AND FATTENING, TO NAME JUST A FEW OF THE SHORTCOMINGS OF THE MATHEMATICAL SYSTEM. I HAPPENED ON IT QUITE BY ACCIDENT. SHE WAS SUFFERING THROUGH A MAKE-UP TEST WHEN I WALKED BY. OLD MATH TEACHER THAT I AM, I COULDN'T RESIST BUTTING IN. I'M NOT SURE I WAS A HELP, BUT IT DID REMIND ME OF MY LOST YOUTH.

Time was when I tutored every afternoon. It wasn't that I left my Houston school refreshed after an eight-hour teaching day and skipped into the setting sun determined to give my time to the disadvantaged of the city. That would have been a noble gesture, but like most noble gestures, you have to be able to afford it. I couldn't. Unabashed, I tutored for the money. Anyone who taught school in the sixties understands that.

I didn't take folks off the streets. I knew the students and their parents and knew success was lurking there, no matter how deeply hidden. Good genes or not, they were often a pretty hardcore lot. It was the age of (1) "I do my own thing"; and (2) "If my peers feel it's right and I like the way it feels, then it is right"; and (3) "I don't believe in establishment values." I guess things haven't changed all that much.

The problem with femme soles plugging out a living teaching is that they lose patience with that kind of thinking somewhere between the paycheck and the Neiman's bill. We further find our patience wearing a little thin over the excuse of "minimal learning disability." Find me someone who doesn't have one. I expect I am as severely handicapped as anyone on the block. I still have to read everything at least twice. I passed a door in the Edinburgh airport this summer which had a sign that read "Push bar to open." I read it "Push to open bar." Thinking the suggestion had merit, I did. Horns and whistles went off everywhere. I covered by speaking only French to the attendant who came to survey the problem. Given the quality of my French, he probably thought he had a Swahili on his hands. In any case, I escaped.

In the old days, if I hurried I could get home from school at 4 P.M. I tutored 4:00 to 5:00 and 5:00 to 6:00. About half the time I got dinner thrown into the tutoring fee. I was too tired to cook. I was also too tired to put up with much nonsense or many excuses. We did it. We did it then and we did it until it all became clear, their apathy, Little League practice, and my errands notwithstanding. Sometimes their mamas had to do my grocery shopping, but grammar and math got done.

Through the party season I had occasion to visit with six of my former tutoring students. They have all graduated from college. They are all successful in their chosen fields. One is a lawyer, one a CPA, one holds a job with Dresser Industries, one runs a well-known summer camp, and one has just received his Ph.D. The count goes on.

The nicest thing about it is that they all seem to remember the experience fondly. One reminded me of the time he announced he was running away from home. We had an hour session on how one supports a TransAm on the salary of a fry cook at the local hamburger stand. There is a lot to be said for primitive economics. I didn't mess around much with Veblen. I went with the crap-table theory. If you don't put it down you can't pick it up. You can get economics through to a junior high student in an Izod shirt that way.

I used very little philosophy, except Hegel who said, "I have surveyed the field and I know." I did use a lot of positive reinforcement because when they got it right I really was excited and proud — not to mention tired and relieved. We forged a very close bond.

The nice part about advancing old age is that your successful students advance you from chief to guru, and pay their dues by seeing that at parties your glass remains full and that you stay on the dance floor until what they consider unladylike music presents itself. I could dance that, too, but they won't let me.

I love every minute of their success, and glory in the fact that I'm going to have the most famous and successful batch of wheelchair pushers at the old folks home. One mother said to me this week, "If you can just hang in long enough everything will be okay." She's right. My phone rings daily with former students on the line asking where they ought to send their children to school. I love it. My advice is to find a teacher who likes teaching enough to give up after-school tennis, isn't swayed by relative values and educational fads, and never quits calling cadence. It may not be a modern method of education, but it works.

"By their fruits shall ye know them . . .", and I am proud of this crop. That's the real payoff of teaching school, and if you can hang in long enough, it always comes.

31

IT HAS HAPPENED TWICE RECENTLY. I DON'T UNDER-
STAND IT. TODAY, AFTER A HARASSING SEVEN-HOUR
DAY, I LEFT SCHOOL AND RAN ERRANDS ON THE WAY
HOME. AS LI'L ABNER USED TO PHRASE IT, "LIKE ANY RED-
BLOODED AMERICAN GIRL WOULD DO."

I was in the neighborhood supermarket when I was
hailed by several of my vacationing students. Their mothers
were pushing the carts.

"Hello, Budgie," one mother said. "I never expected
to see you in the grocery store. Somehow I always expect to
see you with papers in hand or a phone at your ear."

It's true that I find myself in that posture often, but
it isn't congenital. I could understand it if I looked like Jack
Spratt, but I don't. I look like Mrs. Spratt, and you don't
arrive at that state of grace without habitual trips to the grocery store. I wonder how they think I manage.

I can see it all now. The alarm goes off some Monday
morning at 6:30 A.M. and I pick up the phone and say,
"Waldorf Astoria? Room Service? Please send an English
muffin and two strips of crisp bacon to Tern Street,
Galveston, Texas, right away." Talk about going on a diet!
Just don't eat until they deliver that order.

It has happened at the cleaners, too. I smiled sweetly
and did not point out that I wear clean clothes often. If I
were not at the cleaners, I would be bending over the washing machine. That should give them pause.

I could probably cover the deficit selling tickets to
see me running the vacuum or mowing the lawn. It would
require ear plugs for my performance putting things back

together with the hot-glue gun or unstopping the drain. I'm not too good at plumbing. Stomping down those wayward shingles on the roof that never really set tests my vocabulary to its fullest. It's not so much the stomping. It's hoisting myself up on the roof to get in stomping stance that tests me. I've ordered one of those hundred-dollar ladders that bends in the middle that I found in the gasoline bill. It might help if I could figure out how to put it together.

Maybe I can get help. I often do. When I found myself on my back on the dining-room floor last week pushing with both feet and both arms, trying to extend the table so I could add another leaf for supper club, I decided God didn't mean for headmistresses to find themselves in this state. I called loudly to my neighbor/ex-Board President/travel business partner and suggested that he and his wife might consider joining me in this one more venture before I ran amok in the streets. Mercifully, they did.

I realize that sometimes students have a warped idea of how headmistresses live. Until recently I never suspected their parents did also. Even if I'm not climbing on the roof or cutting the grass, it is highly unlikely that I am sitting among a staff of servants waiting for one of them to peel me a grape.

I can be just as imperial as the next bear when called upon, but I am rarely imperial out of season. Perhaps it goes with the territory, this perceived image. Perhaps I am failing to live up to the proper standard. Perhaps the standard desired image is patently ridiculous.

As I was creating my cold meat loaf sandwich for lunch tomorrow, I dropped and broke a jar of mustard all over the kitchen floor. "Hello? Waldorf? Housekeeping, please. Would you send the maid to my suite right away, please? There is mustard on my floor!" I *wish*!

32

OH LORD, IT'S HARD TO GET READY FOR A STORM.
AFTER YOU'VE GOTTEN THE STORM BLINDS UP
— WHICH AIN'T EASY FOR A FAT LITTLE GRAY-
HEADED HEADMISTRESS BECAUSE THE AVAILABLE HELP
IS USUALLY OFF PUTTING UP THEIR OWN STORM BLINDS
— AND BROUGHT IN ALL THE POT PLANTS OFF THE
PORCHES, AND SECURED ALL POSSIBLE FLYING DEBRIS,
THE HARD PART COMES.

This is a big bad sonovagun killer storm. We may not
come back to find house, school, hair, hide or anything.
What are you going to take with you? One car. One crowded
highway. Anyone pulling a trailer is certifiably insane.
Choose. Be judicious. What in your life is really worth saving? Everything and nothing.

Okay. Secure the silver in the vault. If looters break
into it, it will blow them up. There is gunpowder in the
walls. Take clothes. Usable ones to wear during the storm,
or your new winter wardrobe which it's too hot to wear
until November? Jewelry? Certainly. Guns? Sure. What else
protects the jewelry? Personal papers? Of course, but which
ones? Ever try to do your income tax with no records? Pictures? You can live without those, but what a shame to lose
those good Morocco shots. I guarantee you I'm not going
there again. They've got snakes in the souks. I don't do
snakes. Better save the pictures. And what about China? You
going there again soon? But everything can't go. It won't fit.

I've done it. I've decided. I've put all the past
"Hickory Sticks" in a waterproof garbage sack. They probably feel right at home there. Perhaps on top of the bed they

135

will escape the storm surge and I can foist them off on posterity. The pictures are in a different waterproof garbage sack. Maybe one of them will make it. House inventory with pictures goes, as do income tax files and doctoral work. Clothes — a judicial mix — and jewelry go. That's all.

Well, not quite. I'm taking the collection of old prayer books. They go all the way back to "From Ghosties and Ghoulies and Long Legged Beasties and Things that go bump in the night, Good Lord deliver us." I don't have a copy of the bit about, "From the Fury of the Northmen, Good Lord deliver us." Maybe I'll create a new litany. "From the fury of ferocious storms, Good Lord deliver us."

Any luck at all, Gilbert will turn southward and wipe out all drug dealers in Columbia and El Salvador. Now *that* would be justice on a par with Sodom and Gomorrah.

In the meantime, I intend to meet this crisis in a fitting manner. I'm going to go wash my hair. Then I'm going to get a pocketful of money and a tank full of gasoline and head out. What possible misfortune could befall a well-prepared, well-fortified little headmistress with a clean grey head?

Go find yourself a cliff to hang on and I'll return with adventures when the storm is finished.

33

GOD BLESS RAINY DAYS. I DON'T MEAN TO SQUANDER A BLESSING ON SPRINKLES THAT SETTLE THE DUST — ALTHOUGH I'VE LIVED THROUGH DROUTHS WHERE I WOULD HAVE BEEN PROPERLY GRATEFUL FOR THEM. I MEAN TO INVOKE A BLESSING ON THOSE OCCASIONAL SATURDAYS THAT HAVE SUCH ROTTEN, LOUSY WEATHER THAT NO SANE SOUL WOULD VENTURE OUT FOR ANY REASON LESS PRESSING THAN MALNUTRITION.

That's a condition not likely to affect me, so I am pleased to report that as a result of the weekend weather, I now have the cleanest house in the Western Hemisphere. If pressed to the wall, I'd throw in Southeast Asia.

Through the holidays I was truly the Madonna of the Interstates. I logged more miles than Dr. Tate's Medicine Show. As a result, I had left undone those things which I ought to have done.

I finished rectifying my negligences before the rain stopped, so I had some time to ruminate on things I'd do if I were queen. After I was through stamping out hunger in Africa and negotiating proper arms treaties in Russia and Central America, I thought I'd take on the Hymnal folk. First, I'd find the committee that omitted "From the Eastern Mountain" and duck them in the water trough. It was already Epiphany before I found it was missing. Having properly dealt with those culprits, I'd mount a posse and go after the varmints that changed the tune of "Oh Little Town of Bethlehem." You don't think anybody would do that? Check Hymn 78. I heard it with my own ears just a couple of

Sundays ago. I've grown punchy from making changes. My fingers play the "Minute Waltz" through the prayer book regularly seeking to find where it is that we are, but in my wildest dream I never figured they'd mess around with "Oh Little Town of Bethlehem." Next it will be "Jesus Tender Shepherd" — or is that already gone? I remember when the only way you knew for sure Sunday School was over was when they sang "Jesus Tender Shepherd."

Another project I would undertake would be to make kids behave in church. I'm not talking about the infant that occasionally cries, and is, hopefully, taken out and soothed. I'm talking about the school-age kids shooting marbles on the floor while their parents piously pray. During my Interstate interlude, I attended church in another diocese where my wondering eyes beheld a teenage girl with her feet on top of the pew in front of her, chewing gum and drawing pictures through the entire service. I commented on it to a father of four afterwards.

His reply was, "It's just awful. We've finally handled it by insisting that our eldest take his shoes off before he puts his feet up. It doesn't scar the pew that way."

I don't think it would be the pew I'd scar. Our school puts 350 kids in Chapel a couple of times a week and we don't have that problem. We use a simple expedient. We say, "Put your feet on the floor." No raised voices. No threats. No scarred ids. Just a simple direction in one syllable words . . . works like a charm . . . been working for generations.

Funny that should have occurred to me on Saturday, because on Sunday we heard about Samuel and Eli. That's where God sent the message to Eli that He intended to zap Eli and his whole brood because the children had behave abominably and Eli hadn't shaped them up. It's hard to tell whether God was madder at the sons or Eli. I seem to recall another message in the same vein to David about David's failure to 'splain it to Absalom and the boys.

The problem persists. "Dear Abby" this morning had

138

a letter from a retired Marine colonel about the injustice to children who have never been corrected, so they don't know where they are wrong or why nobody wants to be around them.

If there were more rainy Saturdays, I could probably arrange clean closets, good children, and familiar liturgy, but as things stand I guess I'll have to settle for the sarcastic adage that, "Old maid's children and bachelor's wives are always perfect." As a femme sole, I stand rebuked.

34

I AM HARD PRESSED TO KNOW WHAT TO DO ABOUT THE THREE KINGS. CASPAR JUST CLOUTED MELCHOIR UPSIDE THE HEAD WITH THE FRANKINCENSE. IT'S NOT THE FIRST TIME I'VE HAD DIFFICULTY WITH CASPAR. IN FACT, IT ISN'T THE FIRST CASPAR.

Caspar I has abdicated the throne in favor of shepherdhood. He preferred to abdicate and be a cow because, as we all know, the cows have the best suits, but I was far too wily for that. I've done this pageant before — sixteen times before — and I know that you never let an obstreperous first-grader go incognito. His mama might claim it wasn't her kid up there misbehaving and messing up the program. Her kid is the one who *never* misbehaves.

Most of the time I have found it advantageous to take the wiggliest one and make him Gabriel. Gabriel is a star part where said star stands immobile through the whole play and blesses the assembled masses. Most of the time it works like a charm.

It isn't foolproof. Today we had to hastily remove a black glove from Gabriel's right hand prior to his blessing. It was the same driving glove that was the hit of the swap session in show-and-tell. He was loathe to relinquish it even for a minute, but having lived through the Mexico City Olympics with its ensuing protests, we thought better of his addition to the costume and managed to coax it off him for the rehearsal. There are times I have to remember that theirs isn't method acting and they perhaps misunderstand the role. I was convinced of it when a Gabriel of pageants past came running to his grandmother to proudly announce that he had been chosen. "Mimi!" he proclaimed. "Guess what? I'm going to be the Archangel Gaido." It could only happen in Galveston.

Joseph wasn't exactly a happy camper when we began practice either. He had to be convinced of the necessity of helping Mary on the road to Bethlehem. She looked okay to him, and first-grade boys are not overly fond of walking down an aisle of people with an arm around a *girl* for heaven's sake. Had we done this thing right it would have been odds even who would have gotten to ride the donkey. It's hard to explain the refinements to first grade. The third grade, however, tells it pretty straight. I quote a classic from the third grade creative writing assignment, which was to tell the Christmas story. It remains unedited.

Once there was a lady named Mary and a man named Joseph and Mary was going to have a baby and an Angel came down to Nazareth and gave the baby a name and it was Jesus. Then Joseph put Mary on a donkey and Joseph walked. Then Mary said I am tired then Mary said this is a nice place. So they stopped there and she said there is not any room for us but there was a little room in a stable and they stayed there. And there was baby Jesus. She wrapped him in swaddling clothes and laid him in a manger.

And then the shepherds came to Bethlehem to see Jesus. And then the Wise men came and they brought him gold, frankincense and myrrh. And then when King Herod heard about Jesus he ordered all the boy babies to be killed. And then the wise men told Mary and Joseph to get out of town.

I figure that is about as accurate a report as we get on the evening news. I guess the best I can hope to pull off with the kings this year is that we will muddle through till after the pageant Friday and then they will return to their country by a different route.

141

35

WE HAD HONORS DAY TODAY. I PRESIDED, OF COURSE. I DIDN'T DO ANY BETTER THAN I DID LAST YEAR — OR FOR THE LAST TEN. AFTER WE GET PAST PERFECT ATTENDANCE AND FIRE CAPTAINS, IT'S SIX TWO AND EVEN I'M GOING TO CRY.

Joe DiPaola used to say I cried at card tricks, and in actuality I'm not too stable, but it cracks me up to present scholarships in memory of students whose knees I bandaged and whose fights I adjudicated. I don't know why parents think I can do it less emotionally than they can. I had a stake in those lives, too. I think it's a crying bloody shame those lives were snuffed out early — so I cry over it. I'm entitled.

I don't mind crying. It comes so easily. Besides, it's good for students to see old Ironpants shed a tear. Doesn't hurt their parents either. If you ever want to win a fight with me try giving it a go right after Honors Day.

On the other hand, don't bother. It would probably invigorate me to have a good honest set-to right after I've cried. Get me back on the right track. The track more often than not these days seems to be battle.

I hope that means that I've forgotten my past battles and just take each one as it comes. They seem to come with frequency — apparently greater frequency than they used to. Or perhaps memory does not serve.

There is a motto on the Hollamon Trophy given in memory of my father. It says, "Win with elegance. Lose with grace." I didn't give the trophy, but I supplied the words. They must apply to some other family because I find it harder and harder to do either, much less both. It ain't genetic.

I wonder if that's the times, or my age, or the state of hormones for the Western World. In prior times I would have said "the civilized Western World," but I really don't find much civilized about our world. I have been battered this year as I have rarely been before. From what I can glean from around the country, headmaster-bashing is the sport of choice this year. If I didn't have a Board who stood staunchly between me and mayhem I might be penning this from a cell with a view.

I guess this is a paean to Boards and their unsung service. I don't know why they do it. They don't get paid. If they did, there wouldn't be enough money printed to make it worth their while. About three times a week I meet my Board President at the local outdoor coffee spot. It's soothing scenery. Besides coffee, we settle matters of moment and tell jokes. It saves sanity. Things smooth out. I decide perhaps taking out a contract on whoever deserved it that morning is not the most productive idea. It's unseemly for headmistresses to do their own contract work. Perhaps I'll wait awhile.

They say Boards take on their own personality. No matter who comes on, the character of the Board is the same. Lord knows, I hope so. Mine has been stellar for twenty-two years.

Tomorrow morning before I drink $6.75 worth of his coffee and lay a million dollars worth of problems at his feet, I sure hope I remember to tell my Board President how much I appreciate him. Any luck at all, I can do it unemotionally. Nah, no chance. I cry at card tricks.

36

I DON'T MIND TELLING YOU I'M MORE THAN JUST A LITTLE MIFFED. I WANT TO KNOW WHY THE CATHO-LICS GET ALL THE GOOD MIRACLES. WE HAVEN'T HAD A REALLY NOTEWORTHY MIRACLE SINCE I CAN'T REMEM-BER WHEN. AND WHY YUGOSLAVIA AND LUBBOCK, TEXAS, FOR HEAVEN'S SAKE, WHEN GALVESTON IS JUST SITTING HERE WAITING TO BE MIRACALIZED? WHAT WE NEED IS AN EQUAL OPPORTUNITY MIRACLE. TAKE A NUMBER.

That paragraph makes me a prime target for a stampede by the Four Horsemen of the Apocalypse and a thunderbolt from whoever is pitching today, and I'm really not. You see, I'm a believer. I have just spent part of my vacation in the company of a couple who recently returned from Yugoslavia. I heard it all. They aren't your garden variety kooks. He's a judge. She's a card-playing DAR, DRT contemporary and they both had the good sense to choose Trinity School for a son when that was an appropriate choice. It remains an appropriate choice, but now we consider the grandchildren and not the children. The grandchildren are too young and don't live here anyway, so their good sense and good taste remain intact.

I've been to Lourdes and Fatima and a little-known place in Germany called Walden where miracles were known to have happened. I went as a tourist and not a pilgrim. That's probably why I saw tourist things.

I lived in Stuttgart for two years. There was a lady there *Life* magazine wrote up who had the stigmata. Happened on Fridays. Not every Friday, but predictable Fridays.

I roomed with Joanne Biegler from Rochester, New York. She was a Catholic of note. Went to mass every day at 6:00 A.M. She left quietly and we met at the Officer's Club for breakfast when she got back. I didn't ask a lot and she didn't tell me a lot. I drove twenty miles to Heidelberg for Episcopal service. She didn't ask me much either, although we were very good friends and shared lots of other experiences in travel and fun. Joanne may well have been to Yugoslavia by now and possibly even to Lubbock, although I doubt it. Last I heard she was in Rockville, Maryland, with her husband, my former golf partner. They married while we were in Germany and they have five kids.

Joanne would have gone to either spot expecting a miracle. She would undoubtedly have "seen the light" — no pun intended — at both places.

I admonish my teachers to expect excellence with every class. We do, and we find it. When I speak of expecting a miracle, I'm usually talking about finding a coach on time, or covering the deficit, or having the old building plumbing work. I always get those miracles.

I think maybe I've set my sights too low. Perhaps there are other miracles out there waiting to be seen and we just don't look for them. Perhaps if we did see them, we wouldn't advertise it. We're not that good at hanging out our emotions for public view. They don't call us "God's Frozen People" for nothing. If I saw a miracle, I'd stay real quiet about it. No telling what people would think if you proclaimed a miracle greater than covering a deficit. It would put us in a totally untenable position where your beliefs and feelings would just be out there flapping in the breeze. We don't do that.

It's probably the reason we really haven't had any noteworthy miracles since I can't remember when. It's a pity.

37

I 'M INVITED TO GO TO COLORADO — NO STRINGS ATTACHED. NO SONGS, DANCES OR WITTY STORIES REQUIRED. JUST GO AND STARE AT A MOUNTAIN AND COME HOME REFRESHED. I ACCEPTED WITH ALACRITY BECAUSE I THINK STARING AT A MOUNTAIN MAY SAVE SANITY.

Mama always said, "Say what you have to say but don't be acerbic." Mama, I passed acerbic last month. Passed it like it was tied to a pole. The great wonder is that I haven't been lynched yet. Have you ever said, "Good morning," and it turned into a federal case? That's the situation in which I find myself. I'm going to go stare at a mountain. That's got to be the answer.

However, outfitting oneself for mountain staring isn't all that easy when you reside on a sand dune in the Gulf of Mexico. I lived in the snow thirty years ago. Nothing fits. I'm not about to buy a wardrobe for four days, so I've turned to midnight requisition, or uncorroborated borrowing, or whatever else you wish to call it. I've got a down coat that's too little and boots that are too big. I haven't learned to drive them yet, but I'm practicing. I greeted the mailman in my snowsuit this afternoon when I was acclimating myself. It was 83°. He may never be the same. I had the hood up and the boots on and everything. He thought it was the Yeti. I don't know whether he just quit or asked for disability pay. Postmen and UPS drivers lead shocking lives.

I've packed everything. I could live for three months in an igloo. My house-guest condo is luxurious and warm. No matter. I'm prepared. If the lights go off I can whistle up the huskies and get home on the sled with all ten toes intact. Not only have I prepared for that contingency, I'm taking a battery-operated typewriter. Don't tempt fate. What I call myself doing is refining my dissertation. Said ever-so-fat creation is supposed to be on the accreditation process for Episcopal schools with which I had some say. I find it to be more and more with the history and evaluation of Episcopal schools in America and especially in Texas. I am fascinated with the project, but I would like to finish before my ninetieth birthday and that's beginning to look like a phantom hope.

When the State of Texas declared it would no longer accredit private schools after July '89, there was three years' leeway. For those of us with more than a little experience in accrediting schools, it looked like a piece of cake to design a process and get it done in that period of time. Wrong and wrong. If you've done it thirty times, it's easy. If you forget that you are working with folks who haven't, you leave out a lot of the important rules. If you're working with schools who not only never did it, but never considered it, it's like trying to explain red to a blind man.

God knows they've tried. We have, too. It will get done and done on time, but the volume of work — free work — while trying to run one's own school is overwhelming. We no longer count it or weigh it. We measure it. So far, the volume of material that has had to be read, critiqued and replied to — not counting visited — has run nearly six feet in height.

I use that statistic to explain why I yelled at the lady in the car pool line today who had cut in for the sixth day in a row, and why I was less than gracious to a school who sent the wrong papers three times. If I were to fall off the mountain tomorrow, they'd have to send out of the country for willing pallbearers.

I keep wondering why I care if Episcopal schools do it right. I've got my accreditation. I've had mine since 1972

147

from Independent Schools. What difference does it make to me? But it does. I want Episcopal schools to do it right and better and more often than anybody else.

So, I'm going to Colorado tomorrow and stare at a mountain to regain my composure and try not to freeze in my borrowed coat that fits a little soon, or fall off my too-big-boots.

Maybe that's the answer. Maybe the boots I'm trying to fill have been too big all along. Well, God knows, I tried.

38

THERE'S AN OLD SONG THAT BEGINS: "WHAT A DAY THIS HAS BEEN. WHAT A RARE MOOD I'M IN. WELL, IT'S ALMOST LIKE BEING IN LOVE." PARDON ME IF I PARAPHRASE THAT. "WHAT A MONTH THIS HAS BEEN. WHAT A RARE RAGE I'M IN. WELL, IT'S ALMOST LIKE BE-ING IN PURGATORY."

Everybody has these, I'm sure. They last a day or two. Maybe a week. Mine seems to have lasted a flippin lifetime.

I don't even remember what traumas I faced intrepidly the first couple of weeks, but let me tell you about the last couple.

I took the kids to Mexico, you see. I didn't want to, but *they* wanted to go. The trip to the Mayan ruins had been such a success last year it needed to be repeated by popular demand. Bologna. Nonetheless, I fell for it. Took the little blighters. It was almost perfect until I caught them smoking. It wasn't pot — just natural cigarettes — but I was still incensed. I spoke upon them. I pointed out that overaged, overweight women did not need to spend their Saturdays climbing 45° pyramids in 90° weather for folks whose education ran more to tobacco than it did to history, and perhaps the Mayans had a more noteworthy idea in sacrificing young virgins in the *cenote* than had been previously acknowledged. I had to take the virgin part on faith, what with our state of the nation and modern TV, but it made for an impressive speech. Perhaps I should say it made for an impressive sputter. I was too mad to speak eloquently.

They were abject. They dug their communal toe in

the dust and tugged their respective forelocks and apologized. They even apologized via letter. That really did me in. Their grammar was suspect, their writing abominable and they spelled atrociously. Take that back. There's probably not one among them that could spell atrociously. My kids. Educated them since they were babies. The only thing they really do well is hug on me. Where did I go wrong? Or did I go wrong? There's lots to be said for six-foot fourteen-year-old boys who don't hesitate to help you up the ruin and hug on you.

I arrived home to find that one of my very best friends, my mentor and the patron of the school, had died. Katharine Randall had told me a thousand times that she didn't want to live to be a blessing. She didn't want anybody saying, "Katharine Randall died today and isn't that a blessing." But she did, and it was.

Katharine was a wonderful friend — but not a peer. Then, everybody was Katharine's peer. She transcended age with her charm and grace and wit and elegance. But don't picture her on a pedestal. Katharine had run me into more wrecks than I can count on my hands and yours. She was totally flaky — until the chips were down. Then she had more sense and better judgement than any guru on a mountain. I had opportunity to see both, but I prefer to remember the flaky. It's more fun.

We traveled together often. Traveling with Katharine was roughly equivalent to herding turkeys through New York City. Several years ago we went to the Orient together. I considered my role that of keeping some nominal tab on her. She considered hers slipping the leash. She won.

After a flight from Hong Kong to Galveston, I was bushed. I was prone on the back seat of the limo. She was in front entertaining the driver. About Dickinson, she leaned over and patted me and said, "Didn't we have fun in Hawaii?"

I rose up straight. "Joseph, Mary and the donkey,

Katharine!" I shouted. "We have been all over the frazzling world together, but we have *never* been to Hawaii!" No matter. That was before I learned to quit counting. A few years later we went together to Houston to her granddaughter's debut. We were staying at the Remington. After tea and conversation, I won first bathtubs by flip of the coin. I emerged to an empty room. Shortly, the doorbell rang. I answered. There was Katharine in the hall. "Good evening, Mrs. Randall," I said. "How nice that you could drop in. I'd be interested to know why you are standing in the hotel hall in your black slip with this handsome gentleman whom I've never seen before in my life. Have you?"

She replied by graciously introducing me. He bowed from the waist and left. I still don't know who he was, and she wasn't about to tell me, but I know she had come to no harm and he had been charmed. Such was Katharine.

In the midst of flakehood, Katharine had accomplished monumental things. She had raised a fine family, served admirably in state and national offices for Colonial Dames and Daughters of the Republic, and supported liberally with time as well as money every civic cause in Galveston from the Historical Foundation to Ashton Villa to the Medical Branch of The University of Texas to Trinity School. She knew how to get things done. When I would arrive at her door, as I did with frequency, spraying gravel and spewing venom, she listened — and invariably responded with these words, "You're exactly right. Now let's work on your tone of voice." Hers was never wrong. That's the reason she got so much done.

Katharine had lied about her age so much not even she knew how old she was. She married an "older man" she said. I figure that when she came to Galveston as a Mardi Gras duchess from Waco and met Dr. Randall there was probably about nine years difference in their ages. At the last telling of the story, I pointed out to her that, by my

151

calculations, we had now reached the point where he was 39 and she was 13 at their marriage. Undeterred, she conceded that was probably correct.

She leaped up on a table to hang a Christmas ornament several years ago. Katharine didn't collapse. The table did. The table broke and so did her shoulder. I got her to the hospital. They wanted to know her age. I pointed out that nobody knew that, but I'd try. "Never mind the real one," I entreated. "Just give me the number you use the most."

Undaunted by pain, she serenely smiled up at me and said, "Just pick a number. Be sure it's under 70." She'd passed 75 like it was tied to a post years before.

It's been a memorable month. It can't be all bad when you get home with the same kids you left with and end a fey friend's life with such wonderful reminiscences. In old Victorian times, they would end a eulogy with the words, "We shall not see her like again." There certainly has never been another one like Katharine. How lovely to have known her. She's Charlestoning through Heaven right now — and her dance card is full.

39

THIS IS MY ANNUAL OPENING-OF-SCHOOL ESSAY ON "WHAT I DID THIS SUMMER, BY BUDGIE HOLLAMON." I DID LOTS. I TOOK A COURSE AT THE UNIVERSITY OF PARIS AND PLAYED TENNIS WITH THE OVER-THE-HILL-TRAVELING-TENNIS-TEAM IN COLORADO AND WENT TO THE OPERA IN SANTA FE.

I expect all of these things will be duly chronicled when my mind dulls during the winter doldrums, but now I only want to say a word on the opera! Boy, do I want to say a word on the opera! I want to say $78 worth of words. That's the price of a regular ticket. American money. I'm not sure how much entertainment that ought to buy on the open market, but whatever the amount, *Judith* doesn't fill the bill. I guess you have already figured out that *Judith* was the name of the opera I saw.

In case some of you don't read the Apocrypha right after the comics daily, I'll run *Judith* by again. She was a Jewish heroine who tried to save her people from the wrath of a Babylonian general, got raped for her trouble, and got even by whacking off the general's head with his own sword.

Just regular opera fare, you say? Wagner and Strauss made a good living out of tragedy, blood and gore scored for full orchestra, you say? This is just following suit. *Wrong, Tootie.* This one is like nothing you ever saw before. In the others most of the blood and gore takes place off stage. When Butterfly slashes her throat she demurely wraps a chiffon scarf around her neck so she can sing all those difficult arias without her vocal chords hanging out. Past the first row you don't even guess what's happened. In this one, we start with a stark, blood-stained concentration camp set. Before they sing the first note, a Frankenstein type in football pads, cyclops boots, and ski mask comes out and slits the throats of three kicking, screaming victims in full view of the audience. They catch the blood in a #3 washtub placed center stage. That's for openers.

The next scene, also without much music, features storm troopers wearing English Tommy hats who brutalize assorted Jews, tromp on the Torah, and rape a Babylonian maiden. The maiden didn't seem to have much to do with the story. She just wandered on and got caught in the rape-corridor. All of this was just a little gratuitous violence to bridge the action until the real stuff begins. The real stuff is mayhem set to music — only there wasn't much music. In fact, there wasn't a hummable tune in the first hour and a half of this clambake. They didn't have time to do anything but bellow a strident note. They had to concentrate hard to get in all the violence and hatred. You can't have everything.

No stone was left unturned to exalt evil, defile deity, and degrade mankind. It was pure A R T, in its most modern sense.

I left at the end of the first act. So did a lot of other people. A lot, but not everybody. I wonder if all those who stayed enjoyed it. I wonder if they stayed because mama said it was rude to walk out of a show before it was over, or whether they were sure in their heart of hearts that it couldn't keep on like this and had to get better. Then they would go away whistling or, at the very least, sobbing in sympathy.

Maybe they felt that the critics would dub them avant-garde and sophisticated. Critics love this kind of show. It makes them feel superior. You see how they extolled the virtues of the Mapplethorpe mishap. "What?" they smile at you in mock disbelief. "You think these artistic endeavors are depraved and have no place in society? Where did you park your watermelon wagon, Clyde?"

Ole Clyde here has logged a little time in the cultural field. The exposure didn't hospitalize me. I stood up pretty well. By hiking a couple of hundred miles through the Louvre and the Prado and Rijkmuseum and the like, I gleaned the fact that art is not always a tree and a creek with a cow drinking from it. By wading through about a hundred and a half operas in *all* the better houses in the world, I have discovered that the fat lady's aria does not always end the show. I have paid my dues. I am entitled to an opinion and here it is.

I'm tired of having anger pose as art. I'm tired of paying to be put on by a group of people who can't hold a regular job so they entertain themselves by the artistic equivalent of writing dirty words on walls. If Mapplethorpe and Matthus, who wrote this little romp in the park, want to entertain themselves with dirty stories, have at it. I don't care a whit as long as they keep it to themselves. Sell it to someone who wants to pay for it, but don't bother to share it with me. I don't want it for free and I don't want my money — either my ticket or my tax money — going to support their habit. Because I don't like their pornographic ping-pong doesn't keep me from being a player in the arts Olympics. I simply refuse to be dictated to by the depraved. It is past time for somebody to yell out, "The Emperor has on no clothes — and his backside is not a thing of beauty!"

40

I OPENED SCHOOL TODAY. I'VE ALMOST GOT THE DRILL DOWN PAT, THIS BEING MY TWENTIETH TIME. IT'S NOT PERFECT, YOU UNDERSTAND. IN THE MIDDLE OF THE OPENING PTO MEETING, THEY BEGAN WATER-BLASTING OUTSIDE EATON HALL. SPRAYED ME RIGHT THROUGH THE WINDOW, BUT IT WAS A MINOR DISASTER.

A major disaster is when all the babies cry on their first day of school. That's trauma. Today nobody cried. Let me qualify that. No *student* cried. There were a few tearful mothers. I forget from time to time how fragile mothers are. They need to be treated with care. I'm bad about that, but I'm going to shape up.

One of my lachrymose mothers was my own teacher. She kept reassuring her baby that she was going to be right across the street if needed. Kid's smart. She began wondering right off if we were gong to give her a shot or something. I finally told the mama if she didn't quit sniffling and get to class I was going to call *her* mother. Couple of hours later I trooped the color again. Same kid came racing up and grabbed me around the knees. Gleefully proclaiming, "We went outside and played!" I replied, "Yes, next to buying school supplies, that's the best part." I think Hatsie is going to be able to get her mama bolstered up tonight and Alicia will be functional tomorrow.

Another one of my four-year-olds is an old hand. He was there last year. I saw him in the hall struggling with a paper he wanted in his book bag.

"Charles," I said, "How come you haven't hugged

me this morning?"

"I'm busy," he replied, never looking up. "I'll do it when I get through."

"I'll wait," said I. "Some things are worth it." So I did and he did. It was.

Not everybody is in school yet. Some are young and still practicing. One younger brother was waiting with his mother, who deemed it expedient to buy him a coke. As the can rolled out, he looked solemnly at the big red machine and said, "Thank you." He's going to make it.

It's not all grins and giggles. This last month has been fraught with crises ranging from the installation of new playgrounds to the renovation of old ones. I told one daddy if he didn't send me a load of dirt to shore up home plate, when his son fell in I wasn't even going to fish for him. He didn't and I'm not. That's untruthful. I will. Kid's the best catcher I've got.

Then there is always the financial crunch and the parent hassle. The financial crunch is easier than the parent hassle. No matter how you deal out 300 kids, some mama always wants to friche and re-deal. Then there are those who leave and want you to fight their placement battle at the next school. No deal, Lucille.

If you are the headmistress you get to assign classes and I assigned an eighth grade class to me. I'm teaching Classics and Heroes. Today we did *Beowulf*. We talked about heroes and quests and odysseys and myths and legends. They were quick and interested and have a far better background than I had hoped for. I loved it. It was the best part of the day. Tomorrow we do King Arthur.

I can't talk to you any more. I have to drag out my Tintagel pictures and my Glastonbury Round Table Chart. Oh, yes. Somewhere down the line I have to write a Board report and finish the budget. Drat.

41

MOST DATES FOR THESE "HICKORY STICKS" ARE PRETTY VAGUE. ON THIS ONE I WANT TO BE VERY SPECIFIC. IT IS NOVEMBER 10, 1989 — THE DAY THE BERLIN WALL TUMBLED. THAT IS IMPORTANT TO ME NOT ONLY BECAUSE I THINK IT IS A DATE THAT WILL LIVE, BUT BECAUSE I WAS THERE THE DAY THE WALL WENT UP.

That brings forth two thoughts. One is that teaching is reported to be a dull and dead-ended profession. I propose to discount that claim. The other is that everyone thinks they have lived through the most fascinating times in history. Mostly they are wrong. In my case, I claim the exception. Through the medium of teaching I have explored frontiers that would otherwise have been encountered only on the front pages of newspapers. The East Germans built a wall to separate the Germanies one Saturday. I was teaching American dependents in Europe and had wandered across Germany because the duty train was leaving that day and it was a cheap way to get to an unexplored area. The Wall? Yeah, I remember it. I was there, Charlie. I was also there when Kennedy proclaimed, *"Ich ben ein Berliner."* Frau Leider, my German tutor, informed me that it meant, "I am a jelly doughnut," and that was the kind of trouble one could expect when one failed to take note of the proper German pronoun.

Shortly before that, some troops had encountered a little problem in Budapest with Russian tanks. I was not on the street. I had just left after a weekend of sightseeing, but my coattails remained singed for some time. At the time it seemed exciting, but I cringe at the thought now that I am older and wiser.

I remember being in Florence with Mama when we were congratulated by every Italian in the lobby because the miracle of television had shown them the man on the moon. Our man. I did not see that, although I grew sated with replays. I was over at Ferragamos managing another miracle — paying for shoes with a plastic card. I was properly impressed with both miracles, but I was more impressed when Mama quietly pointed out that she had lived from horse and buggy days through the invention of electric lights and automobiles and radio and television to now, when we could watch our man on the moon. Mama lived through some pretty exciting times, too. Nonetheless, I claim the prize.

I went to Europe on Papa's money until such times as he pointed out to me that he had sent me money about as many times as he had in mind to do, and he thought it might be nice if I found somebody else to handle the bill for a while. The only marketable skill I had was teaching — renowned for being dull and dead-ended in my day. I come from a long line of cardplayers and I know that one plays the ones they deal you. I played them. I went to Europe to teach. And that, Dearly Beloved, is how I happened to be in more places than Grenadine Etching.

I am no expert on foreign relations or on world affairs, so I do not predict the outcome of this day, but having lived through the first traumatic days when the Wall went up, I take great pleasure in seeing it come down. Having whisked myself out of Hungary, I delight in knowing that I can safely whisk myself back in. I was only in Bulgaria once — on my way to the Holy Land for Christmas, but after today I just might get to go back and miss that line of armed troops that bordered my walk from the plane to the airport building. On that same trip I saw Beirut when it was a beautiful and untouched city. It is a sight one will not encounter again. I am glad to have seen it.

This day has been fascinating. The Wall has been breached. Bulgaria has overthrown its leader of thirty-five years. China's leader has relinquished his last office. When I was in China he was still holding sway. This day may well go down in history as a day that changed the world. There are a few of those days. One was the day Archduke Ferdinand was assassinated in Sarajevo. I am sorry I was not there, but I would probably have been drinking coffee in the wrong cafe and been arrested. They would have asked what I was doing there and I would have told them I was just a school-teacher on holiday. They would have left me alone. After all, everybody knows that school teaching is dull and that school-teachers have an existence bounded by books and other people's children. Too bad I didn't choose another profession where I could have had an exciting life. It's just amazing how much can happen when you go ahead and play the cards they deal you.

1990 - 1994

"And as the sun sinks slowly in the west
we bid goodbye to beautiful . . ."
*James Fitzpatrick's movie travelogues
circa 1940*

1

OH, THE PENANCE ONE PAYS! THERE ARE SINS OF OMISSION, SINS OF COMMISSION, AND SINS OF ABSENCE, AND IT'S THE LATTER FOR WHICH I AM DOING PENANCE. I DIDN'T SHOW UP FOR SCHOOL THE FIRST WEEK AFTER CHRISTMAS VACATION, AND NOW I'M PAYING THE PRICE.

I knew I wasn't going to show up. I announced it to Board and faculty and any interested bystander. I deserved it, said I. I had it in my contract, said I, and I was doing it the first week of January to start the decade right. I, said I, was turning myself in at the fat farm. So there.

They blinked, and gulped, and then they nodded. The nice part of being in one spot for twenty years is that nobody really knows what it says in your contract. It really does say I can call 'em like I see 'em, but still I had a guilty conscience. I did extra work over Christmas — iced in though I might be. I raised money. I left notes all over everywhere, but still I left.

Come January 2, 1990, I was at the fat farm puffing and blowing, bobbing and weaving, starving and walking — and calling home daily to offer advice and verbally stomp out grass fires. I had a wonderful time. It was like camp. Some of the campers were even older than I, although some were biding time until college began again. We were all sisters and brothers in the bond. The young ones knew if they usurped my spot in the rear echelon of the aerobics class they were in danger of hell-fire. They showed great poise in never acknowledging that they perceived that I couldn't get my knee to my chin on beat and hadn't grabbed anything closer than my sock on the reverse ankle grab since my arrival. They were true ladies and gentlemen.

I kept a journal, which I labeled *The Fat Farm Chronicles,* that I'm going to send them when I transcribe it and spell all the words right. I had fun, but then I came home.

The heating system has not made a complete recovery since the ice storm. The finance committee required two long meetings before their presentation to the executive committee, who then reported to the Board. The new $10,000 alarm system doesn't work. The Dean of Students is in the hospital and it's time to check grades and hold parent conferences. There is a small snafu with the science fair and a larger rhubarb over the picking of U.I.L. candidates. It's time to do the open house for prospective students; and teachers, parents and students alike are all down with the flu. I may do the whole song and dance as a solo.

One always does penance for absences. It's the 11th Commandment. But today we were interviewed by Channel 12, and the interviewer said he's never seen a more articulate student body. It was payment for penance. All the while I thought they were just lippy. I went away happy this Friday afternoon until I ran into an old friend who looked at me after my great healthful experience and said, "Have you been to the fat farm or are you going?" Awrrkkk! I figured my achievements cost about $200 a pound and she couldn't even tell! It's penance.

2

WRITING "HICKORY STICKS" IS A FORM OF PLEA-
SURE FOR ME EQUALED ONLY BY HOMEMADE
PEACH ICE CREAM. HOW COME IS IT, THEN,
THAT I FIND THE CUPBOARD BARE TODAY?

Perhaps I could blame it on severe thunderstorms or the Hubble telescope, both phenomena of the week, or perhaps I can blame it on April. One of those female New England poet types, like Emily Dickinson or Amy Lowell, wrote a piece once that I loved. It contained these lines, "Once a year April comes over the hill babbling like an idiot and strewing flowers."

Well, it did. I am not sure how much I can blame on April and how much accrues to just plain living. Maybe that should read "working for a living." Most people work for a living. If they don't work, either in the home or out of it, perhaps they might consider it. It might make both my taxes and my stress level decline. I would look fondly on that.

I have a secret weapon for stress level. I go to the golf course. I don't go for tournaments or lessons or low scores. I go late in the afternoon, alone, when there are few people on the course to demand that I play fast, or slow, and I tee that sucker up and knock the cover off it. If it doesn't go where I want it to I tee up another one and knock the cover off it. Then I amble down the fairway and listen to the surf and watch the birds, and explain to God that I would appreciate it if He would pay a little more attention because I am not getting all the help I need.

I was driving home from one of my many out-of-town engagements last week (Tonto says they are going to have to get a heating pad to keep my chair warm) and considering why it might be that I needed so much help. After all, I am sound of wind and limb. I have a plentitude of experience in my chosen field. I am not overburdened with personal economic problems. I have almost no responsibilities except to myself, my church and my school. I have already fulfilled those others. There is no guilt residual. So how come I get stressed out?

My day is no different from anybody else's, but I know about my day. Let's take it for an example. "A Day in the Life of a Headmistress." Maybe we will go for 48 hours. That seems to be a popular show.

WEDNESDAY MORNING: Funny thing. I barely remember Wednesday morning. Parent conference. Teacher interview. May Fete practice. Another teacher interview. Prospective parent tour of the school. Conference with colleague over accreditation — long conference. Conference with Board President — routine. Conference with architect over new building which came in too high. Conference with prospective contractor over possible cuts. Finish 1990-1991 budget after setting salaries. First grade comes to show me *Wizard of Oz* pictures. PR lady calls to set up pictures for *Soundings* winners. Proof newsletter. Meet with new lady handling endowment fund. With all the bank changes, I want to make sure she knows what it is we want. Write May Fete speech. Write speech for Trinity School Sunday. Go to dressmaker, doctor, cleaners, bank, grocery store, and filling station. Be ready to go to dinner at 7:30, smiling, with head washed and nails patched.

THURSDAY: Parent conference at 8:00 A.M. She didn't show. Arrived late to chapel. Pre-school looks at me accusingly. May Fete practice. The Earth Day people want me to give up the balloons that have been a symbol of May Fete for over 20 years in favor of something biodegradable. I do not express to Earth Day people how I feel about their intervention. Call from Board President — we have to get to the Appraisal District office this very day to get form to declare new building a tax-exempt entity prior to April 30. CAD is in LaMarque. History teacher wants me to arrange exhibit space for our "Time Magazine, January 1, 1600" at the library. Can do if I will throw in some class for a video taping session for one of their promotional films. Good for us both. We are norming a standardized test for the Psychological Corporation of America. Testing time. Be quiet. Mail comes. There are three forms from other schools asking our help in solving their problems. One form is from a graduate student. I notice that she can neither write nor spell the English language. I determine that she needs more help than I can give and toss the form. A lady, former parent who has been very helpful to the school, needs help for a friend on which boarding school might be best for her nephew. We drag out books. It takes the better part of an hour.

There is nothing in the above list that should cause trauma. The storm is not severe and the grass needs the rain. I got the clothes from the cleaners in time, and the flowerbeds weeded, and I don't have to cook. I'm going out to eat a Maxiburger, my favorite meal. Nothing stressful, but it is like being nibbled to death by barracuda. I bet each and every one of you have had exactly the same kind of day. Let me recommend to you a little time on the tee just as soon as the course dries out. Even if the Lord won't do anything about your hook, it is still therapeutic.

Just living is stressful, and it is true that once a year April comes over the hill babbling like an idiot and strewing flowers. Next year I plan to have time to smell them.

3

OH HOW I HATE TO SEE THIS SUMMER GO. IF RICHARD III HAD A WINTER OF HIS DISCONTENT, I HAVE BALANCED THAT WITH A SUMMER OF GREAT CONTENT. MAY EVERYONE SOMETIME IN HIS LIFE HAVE A SUMMER OF GREAT CONTENT.

I've enjoyed it so that I may even determine to drop forty pounds with a thud and read the literature on cholesterol so that, perhaps, I might survive long enough to see another. The doctors never told me this was a problem. Les Girls did. Surely they know. They know everything.

It's not that I have quietly acquiesced to the forces who kept hiding the butter and substituting Shedd Spread, or those same forces who banned the bacon and substituted cantaloupe. I like cantaloupe as much as the next fellow, but God intended folk to eat bacon and eggs for breakfast. I wonder where that wisdom got lost. Somewhere along about the time geography went by the wayside, I guess. I'll consider carefully. This is not a decision to be taken lightly or ill-advisedly.

Let me tell you about Les Girls. They are a formidable force. Like the Congress of Vienna, they don't convene every day. When they do convene, look out, Leroy. They have been known to change the face of the map. Recently, however, they have only been concerned with my face. That is due, as the media is wont to say, to circumstances beyond our control. If Rommel had been faced with Les Girls, he would have retired from the field in abject defeat. Early on.

Les Girls consists of a cadre of sandbox buddies that convene yearly in Santa Fe. Sometimes we don't see each other between times, but everyone knows that sandbox buddies are the most privileged of all relationships and not to be tampered with by forces of God or man. Time does not apply. Our convocation, for the purpose of opera-going, card-playing, lie-telling, sharing of concerns of their children and my school — which has child status — is equal in standing with any enclave extant including Lambeth. Only the participants love each other better.

If only everybody had a cadre of sandbox buddies we might not have wars. On the other hand, if they take the butter away from me one more time, it's going to be them and me. Sandbox relationships are the relationships on which nations in Europe used to depend. Wars too. I wonder if somebody didn't take the bacon away from Kaiser Wilhelm. It would figure. They continued to love him in exile. May that relationship survive.

We all went to church in Santa Fe. No contest or conversation. We just all got up and went. On the way out one of our group said, "I was saying thanks that we are all here together." So were we all. If we can all get together at least once a year, we can probably lead the world to new heights of achievement and avoid wars. On the other hand, I don't know about that war bit. It depends on what they do with the bacon.

4

YOU THINK YOU'VE HAD PROBLEMS. MOVE OVER, BUSTER, AND MAKE ROOM FOR A PRO IN THE 1990 FALL PROBLEM SWEEPSTAKES. I'LL PLAY ANY MAN FROM ANY LAND ANY GAME HE CAN NAME FOR ANY AMOUNT HE CAN COUNT IN THE FALL PROBLEM SWEEP-STAKES. YOU WANT BUILDINGS THAT HAVEN'T BEEN COMPLETED? A FACULTY IN FLUX? GRANTS IN LIMBO? STEP RIGHT UP AND PLACE YOUR BETS.

Most of that goes with the territory, and those of us who are survivors have met it before and either thrown it two falls out of three or done a successful sidestep. The real problem comes after you leave school. Let's talk about Thanksgiving dinner.

It's my turn, you see. I'll have it in Seguin at the old homestead which is untenable in cold weather, so first we pray for partly cloudy and mild. Then we count heads. I've invited everybody and their children and grandchildren. The fishes and the loaves notwithstanding, it's the silverware we've got to worry about. If I take all mine and all Mama's and borrow my sister-in-law's, I can probably come out pretty even — provided, of course, the babies, all of them, eat only with spoons. I'm big on spoons.

I don't worry about the cooking. The turkey dressing has been made and frozen weeks ago (according to the original recipe). I'm not doing it all myself, and even if I were, it would be no problem. This chef trained at the Cordon Mama, with post-graduate courses at Cordon Aunt Maude and Cordon Aunt Pitty Pat. For sheer ability to get the "Cuisine Guadalupe Greasy" on the table, I have no peer

— at least not in this generation. And therein lies the rub. The proprietors of Cordon Aunt Maude and Cordon Aunt Pitty Pat will be in attendance, and although you may have thought that in their high eighties they were often out picking daisies, I assure you that when the whistle blows, they will both be cluttering up the kitchen telling me not only how to do it now, but how we did it in past generations. It's hard to function swimming through family folklore, but family folklore is a vital part of this whole operation. It's the reason this whole operation is taking place. It's a memorial to Mama and my grandmother. Mama used to say, "If I don't do this, how will my grandchildren know what grandmothers do?" It perpetuates the legend. That's what families do. I don't know how much of it will rub off on that team of kickball players in the front yard who are playing with cousins in varying degrees of consanguinity, but the fact that they've gathered for some function other than a funeral is noteworthy.

Nor, I suspect, will their grandparents — my generation — be lots of help to them. Last time, a real donnybrook broke out among the scions. The patriarchs sat on the porch and argued about which pecan tree was, in fact, third base. George and Saddam never had more heated diplomatic discussions.

My family were among the world-class trenchermen before cholesterol was a household word, and we treat it with the disdain we have always silently harbored for come-latelys. This year will be no different. Instead of saying a blessing, we ought to gather around the table and sing, "Nearer My God to Thee." Daddy used to swear he would be buried with a package of Tums in his pocket and St. Peter would say, "Well, look-a-there! It's old Tommy. Doesn't he look well-fed!"

But enough of that. I've got to get on with the preparations. It's time to make the dessert. First you take two dozen almond macaroons and a quart of good scratch whipped cream. Add some cherries and . . . . Never mind. It's in the Trinity Cookbook. Look it up. Sane people don't cook like that anymore. You only do it if you're perpetuating a legacy you expect to last seven more generations in that house. It's reason enough for Thanksgiving, and having generations to celebrate with is certainly plenty to be thankful for.

I hope yours is happy, too.

5

I SEEM TO HAVE MISSED THE PUBLICATION CUT AGAIN. TWICE. I DON'T UNDERSTAND IT. I'M DILIGENT. I HOPE MY THANKSGIVING OPUS MAKES IT. I'M HERE TO REPORT THAT IT WENT EXACTLY AS I FORESAW IN THAT "HICKORY STICK." THE KIDS *DID* GET INTO A LITTLE DONNYBROOK AT THE PICK-UP FOOTBALL GAME, AND AUNT PITTY PAT *DID* OVERSEE THE GRAVY-MAKING WITH LOTS OF LOVE AND DIRECTION.

Lots of us oversaw the monumental mound of dirty dishes. My friend Betty Chumney's Uncle Bob used to intone, "Ah, the muchness of the dishes for the fewness of the food." That was not precisely the case. It was the muchness of the dishes and we're still eating leftovers. We'll be through just in time to launch the drill for Christmas.

Between Thanksgiving and Christmas, ladies go shopping with their daughters and also introduce them to the traditions of Christmas cooking. Men take their sons hunting. It's never too early to start, I hear, but we may have reached the benchmark this year. While we were still manhandling dishes, my nephew took his three-year-old son hunting. Zan, 3, approached this rite of passage equipped with his popgun, a peanut butter sandwich, a thermos of milk, and manly resolve. He sat on the peanut butter sandwich, knocked over the milk, wet his pants when a shot was fired, and scared off all the rest of the deer with frequent bursts from his popgun. The larder remains unreplenished from the excursion, but I guess a custom is a custom and a tradition regardless of the outcome.

It's now Christmas-tree-time. Christmas trees are a

hassle and I don't really love them all that much, but I adore Christmas-tree ornaments. One has to have something to hang them on. I put up a tree at the Galveston house and one at the Seguin house and one in my office and one in the cafeteria at school. I watched the city tree being put up in New Orleans last week and would have killed to be in the cherry picker putting the ornament on the top. They didn't ask me.

One must always have a goal in life and at this late stage in mine, there isn't much left that I haven't either accomplished or bombed out so thoroughly that I've scratched it from the list. But I want you to know that I've established new goals this week. What I want to do in life is get all the Thanksgiving finery clean and put back before the holiday ends and, someday before my demise, get to ride in the cherry picker to put the ornament on top of the tree somewhere like Rockefeller Center. It's satisfying to know what you want out of life.

6

WE HAD A GREAT THANKSGIVING SERVICE LAST WEEK, AS WE ALWAYS DO, AND I WENT INTO IT COLD TURKEY. WELL, LUKEWARM TURKEY. IN ANY CASE, TURKEY. I KNEW THE SCHOOL WAS PLANNING SOMETHING TO COMMEMORATE MY TWENTY YEARS AT TRINITY, AND THE PTO WAS HONCHOING IT, BUT I WAS NOT PRIVY TO WHAT THE PLAN WAS. THE BOARD, PAST AND PRESENT, HAD HELD A BLACK-TIE DINNER IN SEPTEMBER AT WHICH THEY SEVERELY ROASTED ME. I FIGURED MY LONG TENURE HAD ALREADY BEEN DULY NOTED. I REALLY WASN'T PREPARED FOR THIS.

This was not a roast. It was a feast. It was my own Honors Day. Just like our Honors Day in May, every class sang, and kudos were passed out, but this time they were all mine. I received accolades from the PTO. I have a scrapbook in which each child contributed something. I have pictures from the Pre-school and letters from every child in school. I also have a big Steuben apple on an engraved pedestal, and pictures of a lovely reception with parents abounding.

It's true Trinity has done marvelous things in the last twenty years, but it wasn't my doing. I just put it in GO and held on. It's not that that I want to talk about. It's the letters from the children.

One said, "Thank you, Dr. Hollamon, for all the new buildings at Trinity. How can you afford all those buildings?" Well, let me tell you, darling, that I didn't do it by giving up my lunch money. It took lots of lunches and lots of miles on the road. Thanks for noticing. My favorite said, "Dear Dr.

Hollamon, although we have never met, I want to thank you for letting your wife spend so much time down here running the school."

If I were a women's libber (subjunctive tense denoting condition contrary to fact), I would designate him as a chauvinist porcine who does not acknowledge that anyone but men are doctors. But then, most of mine come from UTMB and have doctor fathers.

It was a wonderful day. The best part was when big and little, including that kid who has spent so much time in my office I've threatened to charge him rent, peeled off on their way back to their seats to be hugged — and to hug. What more could a body possibly want?

As Tonto said, "You've had everything but the interment." Trust Tonto to hit the nail on the head. But then she's been with me eighteen of the twenty years and she holds no illusions and won't let me have any either. Everybody needs a Tonto. Remember I said that as you are called to testify in my defense concerning her mysterious demise.

At forty you look up and gasp that you've taken on an immense task. At sixty you look up again, possibly for the first time, and realize that you've gotten credit for a lot of good things. It's what happens when you tackle a huge job. It takes 300 kids and 600 parents yearly to help you get it done. It's nice to get credit for their accomplishments.

And my father predicted I'd never hold a steady job. Pish and tosh. I figure I'm about half done.

7

YOU WANT A DEFINITIVE DIFFERENCE BETWEEN GRANDMOTHERS AND GREAT-AUNTS? OKAY. REGARDLESS OF THE FACT THAT GREAT-AUNTS CAN OFTEN SPOT GRANDMOTHERS TEN YEARS, GRANDMOTHERS BAKE COOKIES AND KISS BOOBOOS. GREAT-AUNTS PLAY FIRST BASE ON THE KICKBALL TEAM.

Because I am resigned to my lot in life and stay in practice at Trinity, I am often chosen first. I am considered a valuable asset not only for my prowess at first base, but also because I am good for buying another kickball in case that one collides with a nail in the fence. I expect my popularity to decline dramatically when one of the others gets old enough to drive or amasses enough gelt to replace the ball.

Chosen first I may be, but captain of the team? Never. I am plagued by this penchant for letting everybody have equal playing time — an old-fashioned concept about as popular as an appendectomy with the big boys. Obviously, anyone with this sort of subversive sportsmanship does not deserve a position of authority. I just hunker down in the infield and wait while these little areas of disagreement work themselves out. They always do. I was unable to adjudicate the case of the four-year-old who, having had a snoot full of authority, ran over the pitcher with his tricycle. Must have been looking at the swimming pool when it occurred. Didn't see a thing.

A rule of sandlot sports as dependable as the law of gravity is that when little brothers get hurt they are remanded to the custody of their mother. When big brothers get hurt, it's sayonara to the ball game. Anyone who has ever had a

177

big brother knows that.

When this game reached its predictable conclusion I was not bereft. I had another pressing engagement. I am also choreographer for the cousin's chorus line and we had to practice our dance steps. The average age of our chorus line is 23. Kinsey is 3. Ashley is 6. Solve for X.

Last year I considered myself too fragile for competitive sports because the pressures of business had caused me to be truant from training camp. I solved the problem by loading up the whole contingent in the car and spending the day at Sea World. It was a fun — but a somewhat expensive — penance. This year I joined the health club to get in training early. Regardless of my regimen, I am only good for a couple of days. By Sunday I'm too sore to kneel at the communion rail.

I can't talk to you any longer. It's time to refill my ice packs. I can't decide whether to adopt an orphan so I can be a grandmother, or bribe a friendly physician to put a faux cast on my leg, thereby rendering me unfit for competition. Well, I won't go home for at least a month and by that time maybe I'll heal.

8

I WENT SHOPPING TODAY. NOT THAT THAT IS MUCH OF A NEWS FLASH. TRY THIS. I WENT SHOPPING FOR SOMEONE ELSE TODAY. THAT SHOULD STOP THE PRESSES.

The occasion was the ninety-second birthday of my favorite aunt — one of my equally favorite aunts. She raised me from the vantage point of next door and I adore her. She is a little past cognizant right now, but healthy. My other favorite aunt is bright as a button, but a quarter past healthy. Mama and Daddy are gone, so the girls are all that's left of the older generation.

I have watched all this week the TV specials on the abuse of older folk. I cringe. Surely this must happen, but not to anyone I know. Surely people are neglected who don't deserve to be, but the river rises when the folks on the bank don't deserve it either. I tell myself this is not me. I am not neglecting or abusing my family and I never have, but I haven't been over to visit much recently. I harbor guilt.

So I went shopping. Birthday next Friday. There is nothing on this earth that this lady could need or want that her children and grandchildren have not already provided for her. Mox Nix. It's her birthday. I have to think of something.

We all see her often, although she often doesn't know who we are. Sometimes I am Mama. No point in arguing otherwise. She is Erskine-adamant. Last time I tried it I came out second best. "Now Maude, you know Mama couldn't have been in town. That hasn't happened for about two thousand years. That wasn't Mama. It was me." To which she replied, "It was no such thing! It was a fat little grey-headed lady."

There is no way I am going to take on that mantle if one chooses to remember otherwise. I just replied I sure was sorry I missed her.

But I digress. I went shopping. My choices were among sweaters, stockings, lingerie, and lotions, potions, and sweet-smelling ointments. I had done all of the above before. The reason I thought she might be due for a sweater again is that she keeps giving away those we give her. She wakes after each nap to a new world with a new agenda. If she doesn't remember the sweater, it isn't hers, and it's gone to Goodwill or the lost and found. Obviously, a lady of ethics wouldn't keep something that was not hers. Sayonara, sweater.

Today there are two sweaters from which to choose. Both are practical. Both will fit well with her wardrobe. One is much more expensive than the other. What is a body to do?

I have a course called "Choices" in my school that poses ethical dilemmas, things like having to decide between saving your wife or your mother from the sinking ship. I don't know who wrote it, but I find the proffered problems unusually stressful and highly unlikely. In fact, stupid. Now that I think about it, I will go purge that from the curriculum today. This, however, is an ethical dilemma on a ground-zero basis. I would have chosen the cashmere in a New York minute thirty years ago when she would have known it. She would have loved it then, but I couldn't afford it then. Now I can afford it, but she doesn't know whether she is afoot or horseback now. She is going to wake up some Thursday and give it to the first lady in the Luby's line. On the other hand, whatever I give her is hers to do with as she pleases.

Is making the cheaper choice an abuse of old people? Shall I feel guilty Monday, Wednesday and Friday? She never stinted on me, but then I usually knew what I received. Tuesday, Thursday and Saturday I could do penance with good works.

Birthdays are joyous occasions good for celebrating long and loving lives and pandering to your own insecurities, so I'm wrapping up the cashmere. I want my nieces to do the same thing for me when I am consistently choosing Custer against the Indians. I want them to remember even when I don't.

So Happy Birthday, Maude. I hope it gives you pleasure and comfort for years. It gives me pleasure and comfort. In fact, it soothes hell out of my conscience.

9

WHEN I WAS ASKED TO WRITE THIS COLUMN SOME FIFTEEN YEARS AGO, IT WAS OSTENSIBLY ABOUT EDUCATION — HENCE THE NAME. I CONFESS TO HAVING TAKEN A LIBERTY OR TWO THROUGH THE YEARS, SO TONIGHT I WILL MEND MY WAYS AND GO BACK TO BAYING AT THE EDUCATION MOON. THERE IS SUCH A WEALTH OF MATERIAL THERE THESE DAYS, IT IS IRRESISTIBLE.

Given: The state of American education is deplorable. *Given:* Everybody who can recite the alphabet without stumbling is offering a solution. *Question:* Why can't it be fixed? Does no one have an answer?

Of course they have an answer. Ninety percent of the world knows what's the matter with the schools, but the fixers are elected and the solution is not a vote-getter. Now why can't we just say that out loud? No other country in the world tries to educate all its people. What other countries try to do is provide each of its citizens with a means of supporting themselves. They teach the ones not tracked for higher education a trade. They don't hesitate to inform their populace that it is up to them to prove that they are capable of a higher education. Education is not a God-given right anywhere but here. Here we plead and cajole with those who don't want it and insist that they continue taking our time and money and teaching energy until they fail, which they always intended to do, and then we put the taxpayer on a guilt trip to take care of them the rest of their lives because we failed to educate them. If that isn't putting the emPHAsis on the wrong syLLAble, I don't know what is. We can fix the state of education before next Tuesday, but it can't be done by the gutless.

Shall we now look at some of the more recent solutions offered? If we only had better teachers . . . . So "they" wrote a test to separate the master teachers from the merely proficient. According to a Texas Education Bulletin that crossed my desk today, over 2,000 teachers, who obviously had some confidence in their ability to teach, gave their time and their money to take the test. Know how many passed it first time out? 42. No typo. Four two. I don't for a moment believe that the ladies and gentlemen who submitted themselves to this testing situation were so ill-prepared that less than two percent could pass. Did anyone look at the test? Perhaps there was something wrong with the way it was written. When our teachers come to us with a handful of bad grades, the first thing we do is check the test to see how it was written. After all, you can speak flawless Spanish, but if the test is in German you may not score too well. Is that what the TEA folk did? Not according to this article. They lowered the standard for passing so that the passing number got to 153. Even that is a disgrace. What trait or knowledge were they trying to isolate with this test? The best way to identify a master teacher is to see how their students do. I know. Simplistic.

So let's skip on down to the next item. Year-round schools. This has to have been proposed by someone who has not a foggy clue how schools work. It sounds like the muttering of a Madison Avenue efficiency expert who forgot to do his homework. "It is fiscally sound to use the schools all year long, instead of just three-fourths of the year. Can't let the field lie fallow, old chap, and all that rot. Save *money!*"

Have you figured out how much that would cost? The scheme is to have teachers teach only three quarters. Choose any three. That seems to imply that there would be a new track starting every quarter and, instead of having one teacher teach one grade — or one subject — per year, one would have to supply a whole complement of teachers of the class beginning in September, and another for the one beginning in December, and another for the March starters, and another for the June starters, thereby putting four full sets of teachers on the payroll instead of one.

No one seems to realize that, for the most part, schools *are* used all year long. Summer is a time for enrichment classes and remedial classes, and an opportunity to take courses that you would like to take but won't count toward graduation. Taking courses for the sheer love of it is called getting an EDUCATION, as opposed to a diploma, and we certainly would hate for that subversive idea to catch on. No telling where it would lead.

School buildings get harder wear than the Indianapolis Raceway, and, like anything else, they need maintenance. Summertime is maintenance time. My school, for example, needs a new roof. We have to wait until summer, the roofers say, because they can't heat tar and apply it while children are around. It's too dangerous, and in this litigious world they won't entertain the liability.

I won't go into the many other considerations, such as rewriting curriculum and ordering books. Yes I will. Do you know that the average textbook costs around twenty dollars these days? Now we equip one track with textbooks and replace the worn-out ones when necessary. If there were four tracks, three going simultaneously, that would be a whale of an investment in books. It would about triple the present investment even under the most prudent of purchasing. Sure sounds good, though, doesn't it? Save all that money, running those schools twelve months. Utility companies are particularly fond of the idea. Air conditioning manufacturers are already booking their cruises. First class.

Those other solutions just lacked a little reason, but here's one sneaking up that is designed to put every private and parochial school in the country out of business inside of two years. Vouchers.

It makes sense to divide up the money and pass it out to those who are going to school so they can spend it at the school of their choice. It is about to become a favorite of politicians because it gets them off the hot seat. Here's your ticket. Take whichever plane you want. Pick your destination.

Vouchers are against the law right now, because public money can't be spent on anything but public schools, but lots of people claim it's their money and they want to spend it at private and church-related schools because they have such a good track record. They say it's discrimination not to let them, and discrimination is a word that craters the staunchest of politicians. They may Mickey Mouse around with that law sometime soon. Sounds like a real boon to struggling private schools, but tell me, have you ever seen the government— state or federal — fail to put strings on money they dole out? Pretty soon private schools would have to dance the same dance as the unsuccessful public schools. There would be no difference. We would all be participating in these frightfully expensive experiments to make things better, but ever so equal, like TEAMS and TAAS tests. I guess you heard that these have now been abandoned and abolished. Didn't test what they were designed to test.

I sometimes think the best thing that could happen to the school system is to abolish it totally, lock the legislators in the statehouse, and let the parents organize education locally. That used to work just fine until the government fixed it.

10

I HOPE YOU MISSED ME. OH. YOU DIDN'T REALIZE I'D BEEN ABSENT? WELL, I WAS. I'VE BEEN BUSY STOMP-ING OUT FIRES. IT ISN'T SO MUCH THAT I DIDN'T HAVE TIME TO WRITE. I WRITE EVERY NIGHT. IT'S JUST THAT MY PROSE DIDN'T PASS THE *NEW YORK TIMES'* TEST OF WORTHINESS. YOU KNOW, "ALL THE NEWS THAT'S FIT TO PRINT." IN THE MORNING LIGHT, IT WASN'T FIT TO PRINT.

What was the problem, you ask? I suppose it can be described as one of communication. Section A of the Mother's Mafia swarmed on me. Remember that 16-foot hornet's nest they found in the Heights with 65,000 hornets in it? I think it came from Tremont Street originally.

Never mind that Section A didn't have the foggiest clue what they were talking about. The Board knew that, the faculty knew it, and I knew it. It still took a month to dispense with the formalities. I didn't have a lot of fun.

Trinity just spent the equivalent of about five acres of river-bottom land to have a visiting guru from Independent School Management in Delaware come tell us in which areas we were not perfect. He did manage to locate a few. Among the most notable was his observation that our constituency needed educating on the difference between public and private schools. He has certainly been proven right. The problem is, you see, when a headmistress spends a lot of time-in-grade she forgets that she's dealing with a new group every year and that she may have gone through it a hundred times but they haven't. That is called old age.

A great many private school parents went to public

schools themselves. Often this is their first child. They really have no experience with private schools. Probably they have chosen private school because they read and heard it has advantages. Everyone wants the best for his child. They want it but they don't always know what the advantages are. Sometimes they hear "advantages" and think "magic." They really don't know what they bought. They only know they are paying taxes and tuition, and as a result they expect a great cloud of colored smoke to float up and a perfect child to emerge in a pink tutu gracefully dancing Swan Lake partnered by Nijinski. Talent is not a factor. Ego is a factor. Money is a factor. Obviously communication is a factor. If the communication is excellent the others pale to their proper place. In communication, I am remiss.

Indeed, I write voluminous parents' letters. I publish reports and send newsletters to 1,500 of our selected friends on a regular basis, but somehow it doesn't do the trick. After years of careful study, I have discovered the safest spots for any secrets. The most secure hidey-hole is the faculty bulletin board. Nothing on the faculty bulletin board is ever read. I could publicly fire a teacher by placing a broadside on the bulletin board and she would show up for work daily for three years.

If you want to hide something from parents, write it in twenty-point Courier in a parents' letter with a banner over it that says PLEASE READ THIS. The Pentagon should know this secret. It would make the CIA obsolete.

But because I still believe in the Tooth Fairy, I'm going to try one more time. The basic difference between public and private school is that public schools operate under Constitutional law, and private schools operate under contract law. In this country it is everybody's right to go to public school. This hasn't always been true, but it has been true long enough for everybody to forget that this is a fairly recent privilege. It may not be a Constitutional right, but it certainly is guaranteed by law.

Private school, on the other hand, is based on a contract between the parent and the school. Parents buy a product — one which the school markets like you market soap. The school says, "Here is our mission statement. Here's what we say we do. Buy it like you see it and take it if you like it." The school presents its faculty and its curriculum and guarantees to make every effort to see that a student is guided and helped to a successful completion of that curriculum. That's what your tuition buys. It does not buy you a vote in how the school is run. A former Board President, a soft-drink bottler, said it best. He said, "When they drop the quarter in the slot they buy the right to drink the soda. They don't buy the right to tell us how to make the soda."

Another thing tuition won't buy is sea change. Paying tuition can not automatically make a student blond, curly-headed or loved by his peers. It can't buy him instant smarts. It can and does buy him the exerted efforts of a team of experts devoted to his success.

If you don't like the soap you bought at the store you don't buy it again. So it is with schools. That's the thing Mr. ISM wanted us to impart to our public-school oriented group. Voting with your feet in private schools does not mean marching en masse to try to bludgeon the school into submission over a program that may be of service only to a few children. Voting with your feet in private schools means simply, quietly, and in dignified manner taking your business elsewhere. Recent events notwithstanding, private schools may be the last bastion of gentlemen.

I guess knowing these things is a function of age, but age doesn't make one any more patient with ignorance or arrogance. I am appalled that doctors who wouldn't let you in their operating room if you had a hall pass from Hippocrates, and lawyers who get the vapors at the mere thought of a schoolteacher trying a case in front of the Supreme Court, have no difficulty in telling me — who has successfully run a school for a quarter of a century and written the standards for all the Episcopal Schools in a five-state area — how to run a school.

It might have been that at one time I had more patience with this sort of arrogance, but excessive abrasion has worn all the insulation off. On the other hand, I can't remember ever tolerating it. Age did not bring me the reputation for not suffering fools gladly. I always had it. Nonetheless, I can't say much for old age. I suggest we all make other travel arrangements and simply don't go there.

11

LISTEN TO ME, CHILDREN. I WANT TO TELL YOU A TALE OF "ARRIVAL." WHEN FATHER DIVINE THOUGHT HE HAD ARRIVED, HE SAID, "I IS THE ETERNAL AM." BUT I WILL SAY SIMPLY, "MEDICAL PROFESSION, HERE I COME."

In my long and varied career I've done everything but tie neckties down at the funeral parlor. I've traveled for a living. I've dug oil wells — usually dry — with Woodley Petroleum Company. I've been Miss Rent Control in Guadalupe County. Mostly I've taught children, and always I have had fun, but never, ever, have I been to medical school.

Maybe there is a trickle-down effect like we hear about in economics. My great-grandfather was a doctor — one of the first surgeons in the Republic of Texas. He went to the University of Pennsylvania medical school after finishing the University of Tennessee. Worked like a slave, it's recorded. I really didn't know one could achieve medical excellence by putting on 50,000 Band-Aids and 100,000 bags of ice, but I'm here to testify that this is a country of greatness where achievement is recognized for its merit. Today I received an invitation to be listed among "Distinguished Physicians of America." Well, right on, you bet and sure 'nuf. To all the doctors that have put the arm on me in the last thirty years I say, "Stand tall. You're in distinguished company."

It's not that this is the first designation of grandeur I've received. I hold fifteen *Who's Who* listings — some of them as bogus as this one. I'm in "Who's Who in Religion." That should strike terror to the Presiding Bishop's heart.

190

I'm a "Personality of the South." What do you suppose that means? I'm a "Distinguished Woman of the World." I don't think I even want to comment on that one. I'm a lot more things, some of them unmentionable, but they all have one thing in common. They were all proffered with an eye on what sucker might buy the book, or the plaque, or whatever tangible notice of greatness went with the title and happened to be for sale that day. I don't know why they kept me on the list. I haven't bought the first one. I'm still saving my first dime of plaque-buying money to wager in next week's pitch game. The odds are better.

Remember when they sold indulgences? That was the middle ages. If these designations conferred some marketable holiness I might rank somewhere between St. Peter and St. Paul, or maybe Judas Iscariot and Pontius Pilate. Anyway, I'd be notable. So much for the good-ole-days.

Once upon a time one used to be able to become an attorney by simply reading law with a qualified lawyer and then passing the bar. Clergy didn't all attend seminary either. Perhaps Episcopal clergy did, but I could safely wager that Guadalupe County's early answer to Billy Graham, Sin-Killer Griffin, was not a seminary graduate. It didn't hamper him any. Sin-Killer saved souls for about a quarter of a century. Made a good living at it too, but it is rumored that had he paid for all the fried chicken he ate on Sunday at the homes of the faithful he might be severely broke.

I don't see why we couldn't do doctoring the same way. Surely 50,000 Band-Aids and 100,000 bags of ice should be good for something. I'll tell Tonto. She has twice the qualifications. She also has a son who is a neurosurgeon. I bet he'd be thrilled to hear the medical successes of the girls in the teacher's lounge.

I'm also good on splinters, and if called on I can mop a throat. Does anybody do that anymore? Mustard plasters? I know how. After all, I'm a Distinguished Physician of America. I know for sure. I got a computerized letter telling me so.

I got another letter today addressed to me at my office, 720 Tremont, Galveston, 77550. It began, "Dear 77550" — makes you feel warm all over, doesn't it?

If you have any medical problems be sure and call me. You might also drop a couple of bucks in the mail to the Crystal Cathedral. As we say in the mathematical world, if A then B.

For now, signing off, EEH, Distinguished Physician of America. Good luck, sick folks.

12

HELLO OUT THERE! CAN YOU HEAR ME IN THE BACK OF THE THEATER? I'M AUDITIONING TODAY. IT'S MY AUDITION FOR GRANDMOTHERHOOD — OR MORE PRECISELY FOR SURROGATE GRANDMOTHERHOOD. FOR SOME OF YOU THE FUN JUST COMES WITH THE TERRITORY, BUT THE REST OF US HAVE NO JOB SECURITY. IF WE DON'T GET IT RIGHT THE FIRST TIME WE CAN BE REPLACED.

I have laid in a supply of cookies sufficient for Napoleon's retreat from Moscow. I accompany that with a variety of libations ranging from milk to apple cider. I have books. I have toys. I have outdoor plans and indoor plans. I can sing it in any key.

"Prince Harry coming?" you ask. Well, almost. This is a kid that nearly was born in my office. There are several of those. This one is now in my two-year-old class and we hug daily, but this is Sunday afternoon in a new venue, and things might not go that well without planning. You understand about two-year-olds, don't you? I was going to have T-shirts made for this first class that said NO! on the front and MINE! on the back. You see, I know two-year-olds.

The reason I got a shot at this grandmother role is that Jeffrey's daddy is giving a paper in Europe and his Mama had to take the other two to a piano recital. All things considered, I'd rather indoctrinate him in the glories of watching the Cowboy game than go to the recital. I'd rather do almost anything than go to the recital.

Even after I have created some of my better roles like grandmotherhood and aunthood, I often have to refine them for the road tour. It depends on the rest of the cast. Yesterday I was pulling weeds in the front yard. The bicycle brigade arrived. It is composed of the children of my god-child. I don't get to see them every day, only when they are visiting their grandmother. Marc abandoned his bike at the curb and capered across the yard with his hand held high, five fingers extended. He didn't even say Hello, Aunt Budgie. Just proclaimed, "I'm five now!" Announced it like it was a declaration of war. Obviously I was going to have to ad lib.

I declared that I was available to be hugged by five-year-olds. I had withstood the hugs of kids five and six and even seven years old, and I was aunt enough to handle it.

He was still a little short of convinced.

"Can you pick me up?"

"Of course I can."

"Show me."

This kid is a chunk. I nearly broke my back, but by virtue of brute strength I remain the Captain of the Tern St. Irregulars.

I'm in the second generation of Captainhood. I was a simply marvelous first-generation aunt, if I do say so myself. I did everything. I built tree houses, and was the unchallenged best at King of the Mountain. I developed monumental underwater capacity because as Moby Dick, with four kids on my back at a time, I needed it.

Sometimes my superiority of mind and manner was not universally accepted by my nieces. Whenever I went home to Seguin I got at least a couple of them for the night. Forget the many extra bedrooms. They were all in my bed with their feet in my stomach all night. Sometimes they needed a little remediation before retiring. Often we had Spa Day with lots of bubble bath. Sometimes that subterfuge didn't work. Sometimes nothing from bribery to ultimatum worked. More than once my best customer, my niece Shannon, at age three and four and even five, stalked down the stairs and announced to Mama and Daddy that she was going home, "Cause Dumb-ole-Budgie wants me to take a bath."

It did me ever so much good to hear her proclaim to the next generation, "You're not going to get in *my* bed with mud up to your knees!" It is irrefutable proof that what goes around comes around.

Last week I had a young gentleman of the third generation visiting. We went fishing and to see the Chinese acrobats at the Opera House and to lunch with the big folks at the Yacht Club. His mother used to declare loudly at every big family function, "I don't want to sit next to Budgie. She makes me hold my knife right." That was apparently a form of torture equal to splinters under the fingernails. I am not accusing Melyn of child abuse of that flavor, but *somebody* taught him to hold his knife correctly. Maybe that's trickle-down table manners.

Scene Two. Later the same afternoon.

Jeffrey arrived asleep at 2:30 and left asleep at 4. I didn't get to do any of my grandmother tricks. He says he will give me another audition for surrogate grandmotherhood soon when he is awake. What fun!

13

I HATE TO SQUANDER. SPEND, I DON'T MIND DOING, BUT SQUANDERING IS SOMETHING ELSE. MAYBE IT'S MY SCOTTISH HERITAGE. I HAVE JUST SQUANDERED A TEMPER TANTRUM, AND I DON'T MIND TELLING YOU I AM MIFFED AT MYSELF OVER IT.

It happened like this. Things have been a little hectic down at the schoolhouse recently and I have been stomping out grass fires with regularity. Some issues have had some substance, but most haven't. It has been a lot like being nibbled to death by barracuda. Finally one barracuda took a little too much hide and I lost it. I came home and pulled out my Big Chief tablet and #2 pencil stub and went to work. I traced the evolution of private schools and parents' expectations from them. I outlined graphically what one could expect from a private school and what one could not. I thought I was reasoned in my approach and eloquent. My friends thought I was having a little white-high-top-shoe-fally-down-fit. I do have to admit it was a tantrum of note.

Many of my faithful readers do not live in the Diocese of Texas and consequently don't get the *Episcopalian* so I have my own mailing list monthly. I mail their copies when I mail the one to Lucy. Theirs is a preview edition.

One by one we assembled at the Argyle for our annual luncheon. I got there first because I had the longest way to come. Ever notice how that happens? One by one they greeted me with the same greeting. It wasn't the usual. They said, "That was the best 'Hickory Stick' you have ever done. Surely you don't intend to publish it." I did intend to publish it. It was already at the printers. However, they convinced me that one does not tell truths like that out loud.

It's unlady-like. I would have liked it better if they had said it was downright abusive. Then I would have known that I did what I set out to do. They play dirty. They evoke Mama. "Libba wouldn't like your article," they said, implying that it would embarrass her, and probably them too. Game, set and match. I called Lucy and told her to hold the presses while I thought of something else that was fit to print. The unabridged version is available if you send me a plain brown wrapper to ship it in.

We all harbor some convictions that are a little quirky, I guess, and I am convinced that when you arrive on this earth you bring with you a ration book of temper tantrums which must be spent judiciously because when you are out you're out. Only "out" doesn't mean that you then move on to purgatory or somewhere and start over. "Out" means that when you shoot your last bullet you have to sit around and be nice about everything. Maybe that is purgatory. No doubt about it, one has to be judicious and discerning about temper tantrums.

It's always good to categorize things. Let's take golf games. So you hit three balls in the water on three successive holes. Is that three tantrums? Of course not. That would be squandering. Just kick a little dust on the first two and wait for the finale to have your real hummer. Only costs you one chit.

Suppose I spend all my tantrum chits and don't fall dead of apoplexy? Suppose I have to live fifty more years always being nice. It's a fate too awful to contemplate. The mere thought of it sends me into such a decline I may be nice all week.

On the other hand, events really did warrant that diatribe, and it was some of my best work. I'm sorry you won't see it. Those in the school business could no doubt have identified with it. However, my greatest regret is that I squandered a temper tantrum. I've got precious few left and my health is excellent. As they used to say on old-time radio, "What a revoltin' development."

14

EVERYBODY ELSE HAS HAD SPRING BREAK. MINE IS MORE LIKE SPRING BROKE. NOTHING I HAVE HAD TO DO THIS MONTH SEEMS TO HAVE TAKEN PLACE AT HOME. I WAS AMAZED TO RETURN TODAY TO FIND THE BULBS BLOOMING WITHOUT ANY ENCOURAGE-MENT FROM ME, WHICH WOUNDED MY EGO, AND ALL THE TV'S ON THE FRITZ, WHICH BLEW MY MIND. THE TV'S WERE WORKING FINE LAST THURSDAY WHEN I BID THEM GOODBY — AGAIN. DO YOU THINK IT'S A PRO-TEST OF SOME VARIETY? IN ANY CASE, IT AFFORDS ME TIME TO DO THE LAUNDRY AND WRITE A "HICKORY STICK."

About last month's "Hickory Stick." I will tell you that George hasn't called me to reorganize things yet, so my suggestions on the revamping of American education are still in limbo. Funny thing, I was in Washington last week. I could have rolled up my sleeves immediately. Ah, well. "The wheels of government . . ." and all that rot.

I had twenty-six kids in Washington with me. Besides freezing flat to death, I had other adventures. Have you ever taken twenty-six middle-schoolers on a trip? It was a five-day slumber party. Never worry about the vitality of American youth. They toured bravely all day and stayed up all night. They're hearty.

I, on the other hand, am a little long in the tooth for this activity and only signed on because there was no one else to do it. After the third night, I became a tad testy and proclaimed manifestos. "I," said I, "being president of the Salvation Army this year, know where all the shelters are, and if I get waked up one more time I'm loading the entire troop up and taking you to the shelter to spend the night." I wouldn't do that to the Army, but it worked wonders and I'm filing it among my cadre of ploys for future use.

I tell you with unabashed pleasure that the sixty students I've had on tour this month all behaved beautifully. I've been complimented in airports, hotels and museums on their behavior, and I beam with pride. One gentleman introduced himself as a regent of The University of Texas and proffered his compliment. He continued, with a twinkle in his eye, "But then, they have a tough taskmaster."

Indeed they do, and they respond to it in a predictable manner. They behave. They don't even seem to consider it a hardship. That's the reason I have so much difficulty understanding all this violence and erratic behavior among students. Children, puppies and young colts understand and respond positively to limits. It gives them a sense of security. Of course they're going to test the limits, but they feel betrayed if the barriers don't hold.

On each trip I got home happily with the same kids and the same luggage I left with — all intact. Obviously, the same cannot be said for other spring-breakers. One was killed right here on our island. His daddy blessed him on his way equipped with his own swimsuit and his daddy's Uzi — or some other automatic weapon. When he got dead due to the wanton use of the weapon, the daddy decided to sue the officer who was protecting the lives of others on the beach. It makes no sense. It makes no sense that a couple in San Antonio were shot and killed leaving a movie theater because they asked the boys in the back row to quiet down so they could hear the movie. There is an old saying that when God created the universe He chose Earth for the insane asylum. It may be a truism.

Where is the limit? Where is the consequence of their action? Lord knows it's not with the courts. Some of you who have been faithful readers for the last ten years remember that I had my own encounter with the violence of strangers. When the local authorities were stymied I was fortunate enough to receive help from the Department of Public Safety, the Texas Rangers, and the FBI. The culprits were apprehended. I picked them out of a line-up and testified against them in court. They were freed by a jury. Not enough evidence, they said. They later did a brief stint in the pen for using my car in a hold-up. They stole it during my attack. That fact couldn't be brought up in this trial because it might prejudice their rights. I'm still wondering where my rights went. My faith in the judicial system of the U.S. went out the window in 1979, but surely somewhere there is some deterrent. There must be something somewhere that people of violence respect or fear.

Young people are *taught* codes of behavior. They aren't born with it. They either have to be taught at home or at school or in church. Parents aren't doing it, for reasons known only to parents. Some think it's a guilt reaction for not putting their children first in their lives or spending enough time with them. Schools in general aren't doing it because they aren't allowed to teach values. To point out that using an Uzi on bystanders is bad form might mar the student's self-esteem. Churches aren't doing it probably because they don't have access to the culprits.

If ever I've seen a recruitment poster for value-oriented, limit-setting, Episcopal education, the present state of our world is it. So why isn't the seam of every Episcopal school in the country splitting? I'm damned if I know.

15

TOMORROW IS A FUN DAY. IT'S MORE FUN FOR ME THAN ANYBODY. ALMOST NEVER DO I GET TO PUT THE BRITCHES ON MY FAITHFUL ASSISTANT, OLE TONTO, BUT TOMORROW I WILL. TOMORROW THE WHOLE SCHOOL IS CELEBRATING TONTO'S TWENTIETH YEAR AT TRINITY WITH A SPECIAL CHAPEL SERVICE THAT RECOGNIZES HER TENURE, HER CONTRIBUTIONS AND HER JOYFUL PRESENCE.

She came to work on a temporary basis to help me out when my secretary decided she'd rather work at Huntsville prison than for me. Since then Tonto has spelled 1,423,423 words correctly for me, fought me to a bloody tie whenever she thought I was wrong, run the school better than I could when I was wandering around minding other people's business, and, most important of all, applied some two million Band-Aids to the playground walking wounded. In honor of that, we are presenting her with the Order of the Golden Band-Aid, first class.

The Parents' Club is accompanying the citation with a Lalique cross, but the school, as usual, can't get its act together without her help. Our Carlotta Barker painting of her cabin in Colorado isn't complete, so she gets a gift-wrapped box of rocks and an IOU. She won't be perplexed at our sins of tardiness. I mean, what else? At least it isn't lost on my desk like so many other things which lacked her attention.

I didn't want to catch her totally by surprise. After all, lots of people will be there — with cameras — so I gave her counsel. "Tonto," said I, "tomorrow morning get to work on time, have your hair done, wear your favorite clothes, and hold your stomach in."

Do you think she might know something is afoot? Well, tell her nothing. When they did my twenty-years roast, she lit the biggest fire. I love an auto-de-fe.

16

*T*HE EPISCOPALIAN CAME TODAY AND I READ THE "HICKORY STICK." I SEND THEM IN SO FAR IN ADVANCE THAT I FORGET WHAT I SAID, SO I TRY TO READ THEM AGAIN. THIS ONE SAID, "WAIT FOR THE NEXT EXCITING INSTALLMENT."

Lots of exciting things have happened since last we talked. I've been robbed in Seguin three times. First day they took the best things. Second day they came back for second best, and third day they mopped up. Sounds like the batting order for the National League, doesn't it? These folks did a thorough job. It wasn't done by amateurs. I bet a truck with "ABC Antiques" backed up daily and loaded up. Those things taken were branding-irons and old iron pots that had been on the trail drives and one rocking chair that was made for my ever-so-great Aunt May at the penitentiary at Huntsville because she was too great to sit in a normal chair. It's an eyewitness fact that she displaced so much water she could float sitting up.

But those treasures are all gone now. Old 100-pound iron pots sitting on the upstairs porch for a century are gone because some antique dealer had a sale for them. Figured he might as well take them. They were obviously free. Not his, but not contested.

I went home to contest. I was traveling light — schooner-rigged. I had a toothbrush and a sawed-off shotgun. Unfortunately, I only got to use the toothbrush.

One of the reasons I got short shrift in the investigative realm was that the same weekend there was the murdered, stabbed body of a fourteen-year-old girl left on the steps of St. Andrew's Episcopal Church. With the police department's limited resources, it's first things first.

I've just gotten a phone call from my best sandpile buddy now living in Mississippi. She began, "What are you doing?" I replied, "Changing the sprinkler in the front yard and eating an ice cream bar."

It's all so normal in a totally abnormal world. I shouldn't have been changing the sprinkler and sighing over loss. I should have been mounting a posse and pursuing the lily-livered sons of perdition. I should have been running them to ground and taking revenge — whether I recovered my stuff or not.

"Vengeance is mine sayeth the Lord." Well, it's mine too, Lord, when you haven't got time to sweat the small stuff. And I'm not sure either one of us is doing his job.

Police are overworked, underpaid and under-appreciated. When they do their jobs and catch somebody, somebody else turns them loose. And the rest of us move and change the sprinkler and eat an ice cream bar.

It's disgusting, the complacency of the judiciary and yours and mine. Next time I get hit I'm mounting up. I'm going to go get my culprit and I intend to show no mercy, but I'm not out to save the world — just to save my stuff. Unless you mount up with me I'm going to leave your problems alone. If you want to get shot on the freeway, go ahead. If you want to have your children accosted on the way to school, go ahead. If you want your generations-old family belongings appropriated just because somebody else wants them, go ahead. Vengeance may be Yours, Lord, but maybe You ought to deputize me, 'cause I'm tired of waiting. I'm mounting up — and, as the old saying goes, let the devil take the hindmost.

17

T O: HEADS OF SCHOOLS
AND OTHER INTERESTED BYSTANDERS
FROM: BUDGIE

I shall begin this in the time-honored tradition of all good Texas tales . . . "You ain't gonna believe this, but . . . "

But — the Board of Trinity has met and determined that I'm a high ticket item in a short fall budget, and the school probably needs a new direction anyway, so perhaps the better part of valor is to ask me to take early retirement.

I have to tell you that I was absolutely blind sided by this December 1st action, and it's taken me awhile to reach a level enough posture to tell you about it in person. I did write a quick letter in December saying the usual apocryphal things. You know the drill.

"I've loved my twenty-four years here at Trinity, but the fact of the matter is that I always dreamed of having a kumquat farm in South Saudi Arabia, and I hear this is a bumper kumquat year in Kuwait, so please accept my early retirement so I can take advantage of the market."

I explained to the Executive Committee that the standard procedure was to face it with a letter from the Board thanking me for my twenty-four years of service and wishing me well in the kumquat venture. I left for Christmas thinking it would be forthcoming.

You have to understand that this Board, from their vast experience, knows how to do everything. On the decision-making committee of sixteen, eight of them have served on the Board only since August, and the full average tenure is 2.3 years. In their wisdom, they decided to wait "until a more auspicious time." I don't know when. When Halley's comet returns, perhaps.

Forgive them. They really mean well. They just haven't been to Trustee Dancing School and they don't know the steps. Their failure to do this was truly not meant as an added insult to me. But since the letter is obviously not going to be forthcoming in a timely manner, Dick Ekdahl, Bill Scheel, Gloria Snyder, and Liz Barnes thought I ought to say something to you myself. I thought they were right.

Early on in my tenure I went to Miss Ima Hogg's ninetieth birthday bash and was seated next to a trustee of St. Stephen's. I was asking why in life an honored head had chosen to retire. The trustee's comment to me was, "Budgie, sooner or later everybody runs out of string. You will too." Bingo. I pass that wisdom on to you with my endorsement and the sincere hope that you will be able to gauge the length of your string better than I did.

There is an award at Trinity called the Hollamon Award given in memory of my father. It's for outstanding lower school student. I was asked back then what inscription I thought would be fitting. I chose one my family has used for generations. It says:

Fight your fight.

Run your race.

Win with elegance.

Lose with grace.

I'm striving to live up to that in spite of the wound in my ego that measures about four feet by ten. The many supportive and loving messages from those of you who knew have helped immeasurably.

Because I don't want to embarrass you by having to appear as character witnesses, I promise you that unless I just absolutely, positively have to do otherwise, I will keep my shotgun graciously unloaded.

We Hollamons always land on our feet. I expect to

be around to continue the long and valuable friendships we have had through these twenty-four years. This old broad may be out of string, but she's not comatose.

And in the time-honored closing of all good Texas tales, I end with "And that's no B—s—t!"

With much love,
Budgie Hollamon

18

OLE TONTO IS GONE. LEFT THIS WEEK. IF OLE TONTO HAD BEEN HERE TYPING, CORRECTING AND EDITORIALIZING ON "HICKORY STICK" AS SHE DID THE TWENTY YEARS WE WROTE THEM, SHE'D CALL THAT A PUSILLANIMOUS OPENING. SHE'D MARVEL AT THE FACT THAT WITH MY JOHN WAYNE HERITAGE, I DIDN'T SLAM 'EM WITH "AND ANOTHER REDSKIN BIT THE DUST."

Of course, Ole Tonto wasn't a redskin so she didn't worry about tribal retribution and such. She had a real name. It was Winifred Louise Ansell (Mrs. Lee B.), as we used to say in the old newspaper game. She had a husband and four sons — all going straight — all even illustrious instead of notorious as we used to fear when they were young. She was also proud of her four daughters-in-law and three pews full of grandchildren. She had a helper named Chatty who used to say "Mrs. Ansell, we done good. There ain't a hood in the bunch." That, in itself, is some kind of fame.

Wini had already served her time as president of the Junior League, president of the Women of the Church and president of the Pearl Diving Daughters of the Blue Stocking Mothers of the War of 1812 — or whatever. I guess that's why she volunteered, after a cocktail party conversation, to come help me for a few days until I found a suitable administrative assistant. The search lasted twenty-two years and I never found anyone more suited to the position. After about five years she just accepted her fate.

For twelve of those twenty-two years we ran the school alone. Some days we ran it better than others. I would

208

write lofty edicts and Wini would see that the words were spelled right before they hit the streets. I'd write indignant letters to unfortunate offenders and Wini would see that they never found their way to the post office. I'd lose it. She'd find it. Those were good years and we were a good team, the Lone Ranger and Tonto. The school flourished.

The name stuck to her — if not to me. Back in the days of CB's in cars when everybody had a "moniker," Tonto was hers. I never had one because I never figured out how one worked the CB. The moniker was picked up around the school world. Heads of schools would call and say, "Is that you, Tonto?" Often, they just talked to her. Might as well. She knew the answers.

When I left in January my keys to the kingdom were placed in her hands. There were never more loyal hands. The last present she placed in my hands was her 300-copy packet of "Hickory Sticks" she'd saved in case we ever wrote a book. The last time I heard that she was up out of the bed was when she heard somebody had removed my twenty-years-as-headmistress portrait from the wall, but she relaxed against the pillows when she was assured that the new head had discovered its absence and he and the faculty had searched for it, found it and replaced it. Some call that loyalty. In good South Texas parlance, it's called standing hitched. It is a rare quality in today's world.

This morning I got a call from Carol Barnwell telling me it was my month in the barrel for "Hickory Stick." I reminded her I no longer resided in the Diocese of Texas — was, in fact, Interim Head of TMI, the Diocesan school for West Texas. Carol said never mind the details. Get to writing. I could hear Wini, who had to remind me monthly, say "Well, when are you going to get around to that? Some Thursday?"

Right, Tonto. It's Thursday.

1994 - 1995

The TMI Experience

The Sun Also Rises

Ernest Hemingway

1

"**B**LESSED ARE THE FLEXIBLE FOR THEY SHALL NOT GET BENT OUT OF SHAPE." I'VE REPEATED THAT LIKE A MANTRA THESE SIX WEEKS I'VE BEEN AT TMI.

Flexible doesn't really give the right picture. For those of you who remember the Saturday afternoon cowboy movies, it more closely resembles the scene where the guy in the black hat fires at the feet of the tenderfoot and demands that he dance. I've been ever so agile these last weeks. Some folks call me Twinkle Toes.

For those who might be a little lost in this narrative, I'll begin again. My name is Elizabeth Hollamon. I have been appointed Interim Head of TMI. I am the first female to hold that position in the school's 100-year history. The media has made quite a thing out of that. It got coverage by AP and all TV stations. I don't know why. It's not like I was going to Citadel and getting my head shaved. I've been running Episcopal schools for a quarter century. I would have thought that a more fitting subject would have been all the changes that have been made at TMI this summer — which brings me neatly around to the flexible bit again.

TMI, The School of the Diocese of West Texas, decided last Diocesan Council to change its form of governance and about everything else it could think of. The Bishop said okay. Even said he'd help. They asked me to help, too. I was happy to pitch right on in there, but shortly after I agreed, the script got re-written. The plan General Schneider wanted to implement prior to his retirement in 1995 called for the change in structure from an administrative head and an academic dean to one over-all Grand Poobah who was both academic and administrative. We had a year to make the change. Only it didn't happen that way.

On May 9, 1994, General Schneider died. I was asked to be the Interim Head, make the changes, nurture them to maturity and go in peace next June. Somehow we got put on fast-forward and made about ninety percent of the changes this summer. Well, why not? It was too hot to go outside and play. Change might just as well be put in for this school year.

So far, besides me, we have new heads of both upper and lower school, a new head of residence, a new admissions director, a new development director, a new head of maintenance, a new chaplain, a new alumni secretary, and some more folk I can't even name. Blessedly some ninety percent of the faculty are returning. Otherwise it would be hard to find someone that's been here long enough to know where the light switches are.

We have a new boarding program, expanded and much more structured. Our school day has been lengthened by an hour. New procedures have been instituted to keep better account of our faculty and study body. Summer school has been redesigned for next year. A whole new concept in English-as-a-Second-Language has been implemented using Berlitz. Berlitz instructors will work with our non-English-speaking students each day until they can be mainstreamed into regular classes.

And that's just what we've done lately. There's a list of things to be done in the immediate future that is about the length of *War and Peace*. Among the most pressing is to find Bibles, hymnals and prayer books for our diocesan school. There aren't any here. Next is to do some severe upgrading on the landscaping. (Please do not forget, Neil, George, and Bishop MacNaughton, that you promised me trees.) Anyone with a green thumb that wants to help landscape one of these weed-patch quadrangles please call. I need you.

So how are we doing? Well, it looks like we're doing pretty good for a troop of newcomers. TMI will open Monday with the largest enrollment it has ever had on this campus. The house count exceeds optimistic projections by ten percent and they are still coming. I don't know where it's all going to end, but I can tell you one thing: It's going to be a fun-filled ride!

2

FEW YEARS AGO, IN MY OTHER LIFE, A BIG SCHOOL FESTIVAL WAS APPROACHING CALLED MAY FETE. ONE OF MY STUDENTS INFORMED HER FATHER AT BREAKFAST THAT HE WAS SUPPOSED TO SHOW UP. HE SAID HE WAS VERY SORRY HE COULDN'T MAKE IT BECAUSE HE HAD A PRIOR ENGAGEMENT, BUT IF SHE HAD ONLY TOLD HIM IT WAS APPROACHING HE WOULD HAVE CLEARED HIS CALENDAR. HER PROMPT RESPONSE WAS, "LISTEN, DADDY, WHO TELLS YOU ABOUT CHRISTMAS?"

Nobody had to tell us about Homecoming Weekend. The anticipation has been running high all month. It goes through faculty as well as students and I am looking forward to it with great anticipation. At my age, having covered as much of this world as I have, there aren't a great many new adventures to be experienced, but this is one. I'm going to review the troops.

When I taught for the Army in Germany, I watched the Brass review troops on a regular basis. Once I watched the officers at Bad Constadt furnish a general a jeep all outfitted in white so he could drive around instead of walk. Bad Constadt was a hospital facility. One has to be ever so sound of wind and limb and agile as a gazelle to be headmistress of TMI because it takes that to stay on top of the game. I guess that knocks out the white jeep.

But how hard can it be? Queen Elizabeth reviews the Grenadier Guards all the time, and in June she gets on her horse and troops the color. I watched her do it. I've got part of the act down, but I'm a little rusty on the rest. I can wave backwards with real flair, but I'm not winning any awards at riding sidesaddle. It would probably take a small winch to get me on the beast. Even in my youth I had to crawl up on a hay bale to get on my pony. I haven't improved.

Furthermore, I don't have a uniform. I thought of trying to borrow one from Joycelyn Elders, but I gave up the idea. I'll just stand up straight and wear orange.

I have also been invited to speak to the 50th Reunion. That's a function of being the first headmistress, I guess. I've danced a collective hundred miles with that bunch at opening Germans, Assemblies and Queen's Balls. I sure hope senility is running rampant and the condition of their collective memories is rotten.

But there is more to Homecoming than reviewing troops and speaking at banquets. There are athletic events in bountiful supply. Food, fun, and fanfare are plentiful, and so is the special feeling of being part of a wonderful old institution gracefully arriving at another milestone surrounded by the new generation that will see her successfully into the future.

I delight in being a part of that.

3

I REMEMBER WHEN I SAID IT. "BLESSED ARE THE FLEX-IBLE FOR THEY SHALL NOT GET BENT OUT OF SHAPE." BUT I NEVER SAID "BLESSED ARE THE FLAC-CID, THE FLABBY, AND THE INDECISIVE." THE TWO ARE NOT TO BE CONFUSED.

I also said interim headship was a piece of cake. One stomped out grass fires, smiled and handed out the diplomas. That ranks right up there with other statements of ignorance I have made. One of the classics was uttered when I accepted my first job as principal. I said, "Sure, I'll be a principal. Principals don't seem to do much and I can do nothing about as well as the next fellow." I've eaten those words daily.

I shall now correct the papers and pass them back out. Interim headship is not a piece of cake. There are tough decisions to be made daily. Many of them are not going to be popular or politically correct, but for the good of the school and those students who do behave themselves, these calls have to be made. I have to make them.

I intend to use as a guideline for these tough calls the basic tenets of justice, good judgement and common sense. Decisions will be made with the consent of the governing powers. That is not to be confused with the consent of the governed. I recently had one young government student quote that as a constitutional right.

I sometimes think that this misconception is more widely held by young people than we realize. That would answer the question of why we see what we see on the ten o'clock news. One young student thought that the consent

218

of the governed meant that the rule-breaker had to consent to the adjudication before it could go into effect, and was appalled to find that it really didn't mean that at all. It meant that when one joins a group like a school which has a set of rules and standards, one consents to be governed by those rules, and agrees to accept the consequences for flouting them.

It looks like some students recently have been behind the learning curve on that concept. The episode occurred off-campus, but reflected on the school and therefore it is being addressed with speed, even-handedness, and without much flexibility. If your student was involved, you already know it. If yours was not, you don't need to know about it. When it's yours, if it's yours, you'll be informed with haste and dispatch.

There are some slogans that apply only in part to headmastering, and I guess the one about flexibility is one of them.

4

I'M HAVING A TEMPER TANTRUM AND YOU MIGHT AS WELL KNOW THAT GOING IN. I HAVE REALLY CLAS-SIC TEMPER TANTRUMS. THEY ARE LITTLE WHITE-HIGH-TOP-SHOE-FALLY-DOWN-FIT BEAUTIES. MOSTLY THESE DAYS I HAVE THEM IN PRIVATE. I LEARNED HOW TO THROW A REALLY FIRST CLASS TANTRUM IN MY YOUTH. IT'S BEEN AS VALUABLE AS TABLE MANNERS. PER-HAPS THEY ARE THE TWO MOST VALUABLE THINGS I LEARNED IN MY YOUTH.

But back to my tantrum. My tantrum today is a good news/bad news joke. The good news is that I've been qualified as an expert witness in school lawsuits, and that little duty pays off like a slot machine. The bad news is that the world has need of an expert witness for school lawsuits.

I'm of another era, and I'm not a lawyer, but I'm also not deaf, dumb, and blind, and I can see that the law these days is so convoluted that it bears the same relation to justice and common sense that bullfighting bears to agriculture. Anybody can file a lawsuit. Too many folk have.

How did I find myself in the witness racket? Well, it doesn't have anything to do with TMI. You may recall that I'm Interim Head of TMI this year. Not a lot of built-in job security in interim headships, so I kept my consulting company in operation through this period so I would have some gainful employment when I finished headmistressing. It is through consulting that I got my insight. See, this is a kind of generic temper tantrum.

The cases on which I have been called to consult recently are ridiculous. Folk can't handle their own problems, so they sue the nearest entity because surely it is some-body else's fault. If the Pearl Diving Daughters of the Blue Stocking Mothers of the War of 1812 were housed on a school campus, even this innocuous and unrelated group might well be named in a suit concerning who is respon-sible for teaching how much to whom. If a donkey were tied to a tree on the same campus, he would probably get named in the learning disabilities portion of the action. To say that the situation is asinine is unworthy of a black-belt punster such as I, and I won't say it. (That's what they do in lawsuits: Tell you to forget they ever said what they just went to pains to say.)

Nevertheless, suits against schools do pacify the ego of some souls, and therefore they will continue to be filed whether they have any merit or not. That's what I disap-prove of, the suits which make parents feel they are "stand-ing up for my kid's rights" whether there has been an in-fringement of rights or not. If parents spent as much energy teaching the kid what was right as they spend demanding rights I'd probably never get any work.

Expert witness or not, I heartily disapprove of the kind of suit that only gets filed for greed and ego. The insur-ance companies settle regardless of the merit of the suit, if it is cheaper than going to court. Lots of people count on that. You know who pays for it in the end, don't you?

Some churches and dioceses are so scared of being sued they are about to do away with their schools entirely because they are breeding grounds for suits from disgruntled parents. I'm probably not going to be a popular choice in many suits because I'm likely to tell the parent who is really at fault. But the blame is evenly distributed. Churches who run so scared that they hang their schools out to dry "ain't no oil paintin'" either. If we do God's work we have to take God's chances, and it's time we recognized that.

Thus endeth the temper tantrum. Thank you for the forum, and have a nice day.

5

PART OF MY LENTEN DISCIPLINE IS TO COOK EASTER DINNER FOR THE ENTIRE CLAN. I SKIPPED FOR A WHILE WHEN THE RENOVATION WAS IN PROGRESS. MY NIECES TOOK OVER THE JOB AND NOW THEY DON'T WANT TO GIVE IT UP. I'M OLDER AND BIGGER, AND NOW THAT I HAVE SPENT A YEAR AT TEXAS MILITARY INSTITUTE, I UNDERSTAND ABOUT RANK. I TOOK BACK THE PRIVILEGE BY FIAT.

Besides, the house renovations are complete, including the kitchen, and I figure it is time we got back to basics. All holiday meals have been in this house since 1850, except during times of plague, pestilence and renovation, and I see no reason to alter the procedure. Stick with a winner.

I gathered the entire clan a few years ago at Thanksgiving before Mama and my aunts left us. They were all wonderful cooks. They had physical impairments in varying degrees of seriousness, but the one thing all of them kept in pristine condition was their voice box. Their vocal chords were forever young. Boy, could those ladies give orders. Daddy often opined that the girls, one and all, would have made wonderful penitentiary bosses.

Each was telling me how to create her specialty which, of course, Thanksgiving wouldn't be Thanksgiving without. I was scurrying around carrying out orders. They were in my way. Mama especially was between me and the stove. I suggested, mildly, I thought, that perhaps they would all be more comfortable out on the porch instead of in "my kitchen."

I tell you without fear of contradiction that I never made *that* mistake again. I could be the sous-chef if I insisted, but let there be no confusion over who wore the tall toque. It was Mama. Before beginning the preparation of any big meal I find myself silently approaching the kitchen like a new ensign aboard the aircraft carrier. "Permission to come aboard, sir?"

It's not all cooking and talking. Occasionally I get invited to play with the younger generation. If you are a femme sole, kids seem to think you are fair game when outfielders or fullbacks or anchormen on the swimming team are needed. It's one of the very few nice things about being a femme sole. The succeeding generations have a hard time pigeonholing you. You get invited, but they cut you no slack. Nothing for age, wisdom or infirmity. I should have remembered that. My grandfather was crippled and we made him round all the bases. About the second inning he always got thrown off for arguing with the umpire. The umpire was twelve. The power of the office prevailed.

I myself was drummed from the team this Christmas because I had the temerity to insist that age entitled me to a base runner. "Listen, Budgie," the eight-year-old blustered. "You can't just stand still and hit all the balls. If you hit, you gotta run." My assumption seemed perfectly fair to me. I pouted all Christmas afternoon.

I'm threatened with dismissal from the Easter Egg Hunt, too. It is patently untrue that I cheat at Easter Egg Hunts. I'm so nearsighted I couldn't possibly see where they were hiding the eggs. I get more than my share because of superior deductive reasoning and sheer hunting instinct. Sell that to a six-year-old.

I'm looking forward to Easter. I'm cooking. I'm dying Easter Eggs. I'm pulling out the silver and the linen and the china that probably hasn't been out since last Easter. I'm going to have a wonderful time, and if I get in a little hassle over the Easter Egg Hunt I will give in gracefully like a big girl who promised to not lose her temper during Lent. But I didn't promise anything about pouting, and if I don't get to hunt I'm going to pout all year. When, exactly, is Lent over, anyway?

6

I GUESS THIS ONE IS ON OLD AGE. I'VE JUST ARRIVED AT THAT PORT OF CALL, UNHERALDED, AND I DON'T THINK TOO HIGHLY OF THE PORT TAX EXTRACTED.

What brings it to mind is that today I donned Mama's necklace watch — the one I brought her while I was traveling as a tour director. Necklace watches were the thing then. It was a lovely little red enameled gem.

Funny thing. Although it was a Bucherer watch, it didn't seem to function properly. I worried a lot. Mama's watch should be perfect.

We were having lunch one day when I noticed an interesting thing. Every time Mama took a bite, the watch waltzed through the chili. I said, "Mama, I think I have the answer. You are dipping the watch in the chili, and gumming up the works — to coin a phrase."

Indignantly she replied, "Indeed Not! I've never done such a thing in my life!"

Most of us have dealt with beloved parents in their declining years. Regardless of the residue dripping off the casing, if Mama says she's not dipping the watch in the chili, she's not.

Mama left us some years ago. She left marvelous memories, and mementos great and small. One of them was the watch which got put away and only recently rediscovered after the restoration of the house. I wore it today. It was Wednesday — traditional Mexican food day at TMI. I found myself waltzing the watch through the chili with almost every bite.

Me, either, Mama. I never did that. I'm not getting old. I'm not losing it. It's not even my watch in the chili, Mama. It's yours. Thanks for the heritage.

7

I N COMPARING EASTER PLANS THIS MORNING, I HEARD A TEACHER SAY, "I'M TAKING TWO GOOD BOOKS AND GOING TO THE BEACH TO RE-REV."

That's a necessary thing for grown folks to do, but I notice that often we don't extend the same privilege to our children. They need time to renew and rev-up again, too. Many parents feel compelled to pack up a kid's summer as tightly as they do his camp trunk. Through the years I've seen lots of problems result from that.

One problem is that kids grow up thinking all their time should be filled for them with fun activities. Somebody else plans it and presents it to them and they choose what they want like Cleopatra choosing a grape. Life usually doesn't work like that, and when it doesn't, at about make-your-own-living-time, we find many young people who can't plan for their own futures. They still harbor the thought that if they just bum around long enough somebody else is going to do it for them.

I have always harbored an especially soft spot for middle-schoolers. It's the best of times and the worst of times for kids, but it is formation time, and how you form in middle school is probably how you are going to be throughout life. I don't care that that statement is a generalization. I can prove it.

Parents are prone to cram non-school time with every activity they can find because the busier the kids are, the less time they have to wander around and get into trouble. That's one prevalent school of thought. It reminds me of a statement I heard a first-grade mother make. She said, "On Monday morning I always give Jack something to show because if I don't, he's going to tell."

I have come to question the "up to the brim and over the rim" theory of adolescent activity. Particularly in middle school, a kid needs lots of time to do absolutely nothing. That's when he continues the joys of playing in the mud, thinks, works out problems with his friends or by himself, and learns to be creative. Watch them. Left to their own devices, they go figure out how to build a tree house that fits their specifications exactly. They learn teamwork. They learn the joy of taking a project from a concept to completion and they do it all without Tree-House-Building Lessons.

I'm a great lover of country music. Opera, too, but I learn more from country music. I think there is more wisdom in country music than there is in the encyclopedia. I don't always know who is singing it or the name of the selection, but I know what it says. There's a song I hear often that speaks about Friday nights in a small town. They seemed to always end up down on the banks of the Chattahoochee with our vocalist swapping ignorances with his buddies. In the process he made good friends, shared a special spot and learned "a little 'bout living and a lot about me." May all kids have that experience.

8

I T IS RETIREMENT THAT I WANT TO TALK TO YOU
ABOUT. LIKE TAXES AND CAROUSELS, THE SUBJECT
COMES AROUND EVER SO OFTEN. I'M ON MY THIRD
REVOLUTION OF THE WHEEL NOW, AND WITH EACH ONE
IT GETS A LITTLE MORE CHALLENGING.

I was retired five days the first time before I took on
TMI as a fourteen-month project. When I retired from there
I lasted nearly six days before I was involved with an in-
service in Phoenix, a Jewish School project in Dallas, and a
middle school project in Ft. Worth. Because I am old I get
cut-rate on the airlines, so I can manage all those things.

Sometimes it is hard for me to realize just how old I
am. But then, on other occasions it is brought home to me
graphically. Today I was cashing a check at the grocery store.
The young checker looked at my driver's license and back
at me. In disbelief she called another young squirt over and
said "Look-a-here, Joey. This driver's license begins with zero,
zero!"

I started to retort, "I can remember when they gave
a driver's license away with every new car," but I refrained.
There's this constitutional thing about self-incrimination.

On my Phoenix jaunt this August I decided to come
home by way of the Grand Canyon. We don't have a hole
that big in Guadalupe County and there's a Biblical impera-
tive that says, "Brethren, I would not have you ignorant." So
Liz Barnes took me up there from Phoenix and I walked
around ogling a lot. I was thoroughly winded in twenty minutes. Stopped four times to rest. Panted like a road lizard.
Thought perhaps all that fried cholesterol I'd consumed

through the years was taking its toll. Then I read the sign. It said the elevation was 8,000 feet and the grade was 4%. I could not pull that combination when I was twelve.

On the other hand, I am consistently shooting in the forties at the local links. Could not do that when I was twelve, either.

My message to you prospective retirees is *stay in shape!* Do road work. You're probably going to be called on to cover more miles and put your fingers in more holes in more dikes than you ever did before in your whole life. Busy you will be. Bored you won't be. Retirement is not a time to rust up or bloom out. You have to stay limber, because there is never a clue where the next thunderbolt is going to come from.

I found that out last year at TMI. I clung to a little-known beatitude I admit to making up. Used it like a mantra. I'll lend it to you. It goes like this:

"Blessed are the flexible for they shall not get bent out of shape."

9

THE MONTH OF MAY ALWAYS SEEMS TO GO AT A RATE RESERVED FOR FIRE TRUCKS AND AMBULANCES. IT'S BEEN THAT WAY EVER SINCE I CAN REMEMBER. BUT THEN, I CAN'T REMEMBER TOO MUCH BEFORE I GOT IN THE SCHOOL RACKET. FEW FOLK HAVE MEMORIES THAT GO BACK THAT FAR.

In a few weeks I will retire . . . *again!* I've made more farewell appearances than Sarah Bernhardt, but this time I may be serious about it. It's been an ever so eventful year, and one gets tired. My last farewell appearance was on December 1, 1993. On December 5, TMI asked me to consult. On May 15 I became the Interim Head. That's not enough breathing time.

Often I have been asked why in the world I took on a boarding school in the first place, especially one in flux. The answer is simple. Centrum Silver may call these the glittering years, but most folks just sit around and bloom out. I had the invigorating opportunity to meet new challenges and make new friends. Besides that, insanity runs in the family. In 1850, my sixty-year-old great-great-grandfather decided the Gold Rush guys would probably pay handsomely for some fresh beef from Texas, and he had lots of it, so he got a troop together and began the first cattle drive to California.

The trail wasn't blazed. Indians were plentiful and unfriendly. Supplies were scarce. I wouldn't have taken on the job of getting 1,000 head of cattle to California if you'd sent me on the Sunset Limited. He got there with all 1,000 head. (Any bets on whether they were the same thousand?)

He had such a wonderful time doing it that he stayed awhile and bought a gold mine. But chances are he wouldn't have taken on a boarding school to revamp and revitalize. I didn't say he was certifiable.

I've loved it all. It was like remodeling a historic house. I know because I was literally doing that at the same time. Every phase of life at TMI has been scrutinized and most likely reorganized. That goes from administrative structure to curriculum, to admissions and development, to building and grounds maintenance and improvement, to transportation. Now everything is functional, pretty, and in prime condition to be turned over to somebody who is going to nurture it for a long time. I can get back to Cavalry Consulting and the golf course, both of which have been badly neglected this year.

I shall not consider interims again. Been there, done that. I shall retire from the field with honor just as soon as I return these phone calls to St. Andrews in Jackson, St. James in Los Angeles, and some Texas schools as well. I am only going to speak at their commencements, or baccalaureates or whatever. Nothing more. Make no entangling foreign alliances, a wise old president once said. You bet, George.